*A*dventure Guide to
Oregon & Washington

Thomas H. Booth

HUNTER
PUBLISHING

Hunter Publishing, Inc.
300 Raritan Center Parkway, Edison NJ 08818
Tel (908) 225 1900, Fax (908) 417 0482

In Canada
164 Commander Blvd., Agincourt, Ontario M1S 3C7
Tel (416) 293 8141, Fax (416) 293 0846

ISBN 1-55650-709-7
© 1996 Hunter Publishing, Inc.

Cover photo: Lily Basin Trail, Johnson Peak, Goat Rock Wilderness
(Frank M. Redmond, Superstock). Other photos: pp 31, 64, 66, 69 *(Oregon Tourism)*; p 110 *(Ron McMillan, Anacortes Yacht Charters).*

Although every effort has been made to ensure the correctness of the information in this book, the publisher and author do not
assume, and hereby disclaim, liability for any loss or damage caused by
errors, omissions, misleading information or potential travel problems
caused by this guide, even if such errors or
omissions result from negligence, accident or any other cause.

Acknowledgements

I hope the following people and organizations realize how much I value their assistance. My debt to them runs across the states of Oregon and Washington – and back again. Julie Curtis and Paula Perkins of the Oregon Tourism Division. Kristina Fritz of the Portland Visitors Bureau. The American Automobile Association. Gordon Thorne of Alaska Sightseeing Cruise West in Battle WA. Thomas R. Booth of Boise ID. *The Tourist Guide International for Central Washington. The Spokane Visitors Guide. The Olympic Peninsula Visitors Guide. Washington State Lodging and Travel Guide for 1995. The Pend Oreille County Travel Guide.* Carrie L. Wilkinson of Washington State Tourism. Oregon River Experiences, Lake Oswego OR. Wild Water Adventures, Creswell OR. Washington State Parks and Recreation Commission. Roger Van Dyken of San Juan Sailing, Bellingham WA. Anacortes Yacht Charters of Anacortes WA. *Visitors Guide to Washington's North Olympic Peninsula. Oregon Travelers Guide to Accommodations. Tourist Guide International for Spokane. Coeur d'Alene Visitors Guide. Oregon Outdoors, the Directory of Oregon Guides and Packers.*

Printed on recycled paper

Contents

Introduction 1

OREGON 3
The Coast 6
  Brookings 6
  Gold Beach 7
  Port Orford 8
  Bandon 8
  Coos Bay 9
  North from Coos Bay 12
  Winchester Bay 12
  Florence 14
  Yachats 15
  Waldport 16
  Newport 16
  Gleneden 18
  Lincoln City 18
  Neskowin 19
  Tillamook 20
  Garibaldi 20
  Cannon Beach 21
  Seaside 22
  Astoria 23
Portland 25
Mt. Hood & the Columbia River Gorge 30
  Hood River 33
  Mt. Hood 34
Southern Oregon 35
  Ashland 35
  Jacksonville 37
  Medford 37
  Gold Hill 38
  Grants Pass 38
  The Rogue River 40
  Roseburg 42
  Oakland 43
The Willamette Valley 43
  Cottage Grove 44
  Eugene 45
  Outside Eugene 48
  Up the Willamette Valley from Eugene to Portland 51

Corvallis   53
Albany   53
Salem   54
Newberg   56
Oregon City   58
Central Oregon   59
The Dalles   60
Madras   61
Prineville   62
Redmond   64
The Pacific Crest Trail   64
Sisters   65
The Mt. Jefferson Wilderness Area   66
The Mt. Washington Wilderness Area   67
The Three Sisters Wilderness Area   67
Bend   69
Sunriver   71
Crater Lake   72
Klamath Falls   74
Eastern Oregon   75
Pendleton   75
La Grande   77
Joseph   79
The Hell's Canyon National Recreation Area   80
Baker City   81
Ontario   83
Southeastern Oregon   84
Owyhee Dam & The Lake   85
Succor Creek State Park   85
Jordan Valley   85
Rome   85
Burns   86
Diamond Valley   87
The Steens Mountains   88
Frenchglen   88
Hart Mountain National Antelope Refuge   88
Lakeview   89
John Day - Canyon City   90

WASHINGTON   93
The Lower Columbia River   94
Ilwaco   96
Long Beach   96
Cathlamet   98
Longview - Kelso   98

Mt. St. Helens   98
Seattle & Its Approach By I-5   99
   Olympia   99
   Near Olympia   101
   Ft. Lewis   102
   Tacoma   102
   Gig Harbor   104
   Vashon Island   104
   Bremerton   104
   Seattle   106
The San Juan Islands & The Olympic Peninsula   109
   La Conner   110
   Anacortes   110
   The San Juan Islands   112
The Olympic Peninsula   116
   Port Townsend   117
   Port Angeles   118
   The Elwha River   119
   Crescent Lake   120
   Neah Bay   121
   Forks   121
   The Hoh Rainforest   122
   Lake Quinault   123
   Aberdeen   124
The North Cascades   125
   Winthrop   127
   Twisp   128
   Stehekin   128
   Mount Rainier National Park   129
Eastern Washington & the Upper Columbia River   131
   Chelan   131
   Okanogan   133
   Omak   133
   Riverside   134
   Oroville   134
   Grand Coulee & the Dam   134
   Moses Lake   135
   Ritzville   135
   Spokane   136
   Pend Oreille County   139
   Newport   139
   Usk   140
   Ione   140
   Mataline & Mataline Falls   140
   Coeur D'Alene, ID   142

Pullman   144
Clarkston   145
Walla Walla   146
Pasco   147
Richland   147
Kennewick   147
Yakima   150
Goldendale   151
The Columbia River   152

Maps

Regions of Oregon   3
The Oregon Coast   5
Portland Region   25
Portland   26
Mt. Hood & the Columbia River Gorge   31
Southern Oregon   36
Willamette Valley   44
Central Oregon   59
Eastern Oregon   76
Regions of Washington   93
The Lower Columbia River   95
Seattle Region   100
Seattle   106
San Juan Islands   111
The Olympic Peninsula   117
North Cascades & Mount Rainier   125
Eastern Washington & the Upper Columbia River 132

Introduction

Rather than just being an Oregonian, where I live and pay taxes, I consider myself a Northwesterner – a product of both Oregon and Washington. Here in Eugene, Oregon where I live – deep in the Willamette Valley, I am admirably positioned to show this diverse land to visiting friends. And they come often, folks from all over the world who've shown us their corner of the earth. With pride I now reciprocate.

But not all these guests have similar interests. Some can't wait to walk a mountain trail, raft an exuberant river, fish for trout, glean crabs from the water, scramble the flanks of a snow-capped peak or beachcomb along a dramatic stretch of coast. Others only want to look. From the comfort of a car, they marvel at waterfalls, deep gorges, majestic seascapes, the austerity of high deserts, the deep blue of mountain lakes and the alpine grandeur of peaks by the score. There are others who incline to city life, to restaurants, shopping, walking in the old town, zoos, museums, and maybe a little night life.

As for me, I like it all and, through the medium of this book, I hope to offer assistance and advice on whatever you're looking for in both Oregon and Washington. I know just the right people – fishermen, guides, trekkers, sailors, day hikers, picnickers, gourmands and folks who go for car rides on Sunday – all of them eager to help. Let's start with Oregon.

Oregon

Population 2,842,300
Area 97,073 Sq. Miles
Capital Salem
Highest Point Mount Hood, 11,239 ft.
Admitted to the Union 1859

Once, driving up the Oregon coast from California, I attempted to stop at every State Park along that dramatic route. It was a happy task, but time has its limits and only half-way to Washington state, after 40 stops, I had to give up. Something like 48 parks remained to be seen, and that was only along the coast. Inland Oregon lay waiting, a collage of city, forest, desert, river, mountain and lake. To the north, with another 148 parks, there was Washington.

Try to better my record if you must, but be discriminating and don't neglect the rich selection of inns, B&Bs, motels, and hotels on the way, many of which are covered in this guide. At any rate,

Regions of Oregon

welcome to Oregon, welcome to a multitude of special places set aside by the state and by people who love what nature has provided. For the sake of convenience, I will cover them according to seven regions – The Coast; Portland; The Columbia Gorge and Mt. Hood; Southern Oregon; The Willamette Valley. 6. Central Oregon; Eastern Oregon.

I will also go into the matter of a place to rest your weary bones after a day of exploring. Throughout this book, prices are defined on the following scale:

Inexpensive – under $45
Moderate – under $80
Expensive – over $80
Luxury – over $150

Similarly, the cost of a meal will be classified as follows:

Inexpensive – under $10
Moderate – $10-$20
Expensive – $20-$30
Luxury – above $30

The 360-mile trip up Oregon's coast along U.S. 101, from the California border to Washington on the Columbia River, should not be done in haste. This is a journey through forests of fir, cedar, sitka, spruce, myrtle and weathered pine. There are majestic headlands, pastoral serenity, rivers, beaches and miles of sand dunes. Quiet towns offer excellent amenities and rugged bays provide the bounty of clams (steamed, fried, or in chowder), oysters, Dungeness crabs, mussels, salmon, halibut, cod or shrimp.

If you're planning to camp along this route, whether in tent or RV, be aware that some parks are for day use only – in other words, for picnics, viewpoints and beach access. The facilites at each park are clearly marked at the entrance. Most of those offering camping have toilets, fire pits and full RV hook-ups. In the summer, the prime time for campers, all camp sites are open. For a camp site with full utilities (RV hook-up, dump section, etc.), expect to pay from $2 to $8. In the high season you should make advance reservations, particularly at the most desirable camps. To do so within Oregon, ☎ 800-452-5687; from out of state ☎ 503-238-7488.

The Oregon Coast

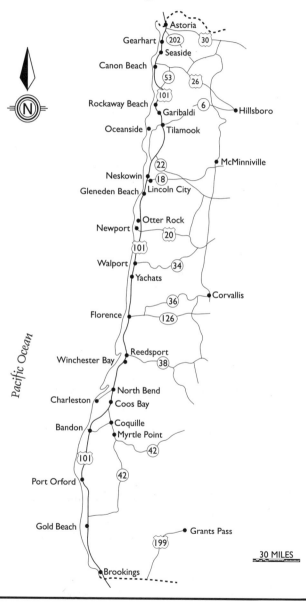

The Coast

Brookings

Population 4,200

Coming north from the California line, Brookings is only seven miles. This town, with its attractive harbor, is referred to as the "banana belt of Oregon." Lured by the climate, the beauty and the admirable fishing in the Winchuck and Chetco Rivers, the people who live here – many retired – are happily entrenched in their surroundings.

There are at least 15 motels in Brookings, ranging from moderate to expensive. All are spelled out in the *AAA Oregon-Washington Tour Book*.

For dining try **O'Halleran's** on U.S. 101 in town. Moderate. **The Flying Gull**, downtown on 101, is another option. Moderate. A mama-papa café down at the harbor serves fine chowder and seafood.

The best outdoor spots in this area are the nearby unspoiled beaches and a pair of parks – Loeb and Harris Beach Parks. **Loeb** has 320 acres of virgin myrtle wood found only in Oregon and the Middle East), redwood groves and a number of river beaches ideal for fishing and picnicking. Hiking is good here.

Harris, only a few miles north of Brookings, is on a splendid reach of ocean studded with rocky outcroppings. Here, there are two sections; one is a camp with complete RV hook-ups, the other is for day use. Locals from Brookings came to these places often. They give them high marks. So do I.

Boardman State Park, a little farther north, is a fine destination for strenuous hiking. Here, against a backdrop of immense sea-worn rocks and secluded beaches, is a rugged 10-mile span of the Oregon Coast Trail, planned to run from California to the Washington border.

Gold Beach

Population 1,500

This town, 37 miles north of the border, should not be missed. There are plenty of motels here but, for resorts with river views and access to the Rogue River, check out **Jot's Resort**, ☎ 503-247-6676, which has its own boat dock. Rates there are moderate to expensive. The **Tu Tu Tun**, ☎ 503-249-6664, is another fine choice. It's on the river and has fine dining. Rates are moderately expensive.

For restaurants in town try the **Nor-Western** for seafood or the **Rod and Reel** for a combination of everything.

Gold Beach's claim to fame involves the fabled Rogue River that empties into the sea at this point. More importantly, it's from here that jet boats, equipped to ascend the swift-flowing Rogue, set out each day. Several organizations provide these services as well as a variety of white water trips. There are six-hour trips (some covering 64 miles, others 80 miles). Their longest excursion lasts eight hours and covers 104 miles. Costs, which usually include a meal at the top of the run, range from $27 to about $65. There are special rates for seniors and children. Reservations are advised and can be made with the following:

Rogue River Mail Boat Trips	☎ 800-458-3511
Jerry's Rogue River Jet Boats	☎ 800-451-3645
Court's White Water Jet Boats	☎ 800-247-6504
	503-247-6504

The Rogue River, idealized by Zane Grey, is a must. It's known for its craggy wood-covered cliffs, serene flow, and its sometimes furious rapids. Bear, deer, eagle, and osprey abound. For the angler, these waters offer trout, salmon and steelhead.

The upper reaches of the river provide opportunities for energetic river rafting and a wilderness trail that runs alongside the water for 40 or so miles. Hikers should consider this trail seriously. See the chapter on Central Oregon for more detail.

Port Orford

Population 1,000

This village on a natural harbor is renowned for good salmon fishing and lures ardent hikers, too. At **Humbug State Park**, they can follow a winding trail to the top of 1,756-foot Humbug Mountain. Have a camera at the ready.

Bandon

Population 2,200

When it comes to restoring our souls – be it winter or summer – Bandon is just the place. The town is uncluttered and its beauty is undisturbed. Lying as it does at the mouth of the Coquille River, the old town of Bandon has a genuine quaintness, a coastal village with unpretentious art colony overtones. Then, too, with its pungent cheese factory and nearby cranberry bogs, it has the added honor of being the "Storm Watching Capital of the World."

Near Bandon on the Oregon coast.

Better yet is the dramatic scenery found along the beach south of town. Studded with immense rocks, this beach is a delight to walk – some four miles of it. The best hotels and inns are found along a bluff overlooking the coastal grandeur.

Accommodations & Dining

The Inn at Face Rock, ☎ 503-347-9441, has fireplaces and splendid views. Moderate to expensive. A personal favorite is the **Sunset Oceanfront Resort, ☎** 503-347-2453. Inexpensive to expensive. We go there in the summer to walk the beaches, crab in the harbor, gather mussels, ride upriver on the stern wheeler, *Rose*, and to visit the cheese factory. For high drama, watch a winter storm, with seagulls riding gale force winds and immense Pacific "rollers" assaulting the rocks, sending spray high into the air. Seated at the window near a blazing fire, this is hard to beat.

There are eight or 10 other easily found accommodations both in town or on the beach.

A number of restaurants are right in town. The **Bandon Fish Market**, with picnic tables outside, serves good clam chowder and delicious pan-fried seafood. There's a deli-coffee house nearby. Our favorite is the **Bandon Boat Works**, near the mouth of the Coquille River, practically in town. It serves fine local seafood at moderate rates.

FROM BANDON. Bullard State Park is one of the best, most varied parks on the coast, a place you can walk for untrammeled miles along beaches, through forests and among sand dunes. Bullard offers 192 campsites, including hook-ups for trailers up to 55 feet. There are also tent camping facilities, picnic areas, trailer waste dumps, showers, a boat launch, horse trails and the Coquille Lighthouse, built in 1896.

Coos Bay

Population 15,100

This industrial town is one of Oregon's largest ports for shipping forest products. Close by, at the mouth of sprawling Coos Bay, is the small port of Charleston, popular for deep-sea fishing, both commercial and sport. Charter boats and party boats are available here.

Coastal Fishing

Almost any town on the coast that's on a river or bay offers promise for the angler. Most local residents will tell you what to do. But for starters, here are a few names. In Gold Beach call **Briggs Charters, ☎** 503-476-2941. In Charleston call **Betty Kaye's Charters, ☎** 1-800-445-8730. In Newport call **Newport Sportsfishing, ☎** 503-265-2101. In Depoe Bay call **Tradewinds Ocean Fishing, ☎** 1-800-445-8730.

SALMON. Because of the need to protect salmon, some fishing areas -including the ocean – are closed from time to time. Regulations vary from one region to another, and from season to season. As of this writing, ocean fishing for salmon is closed and only chinooks can be taken in rivers and bays.

You may hire a charter boat (up to $500 per day), which will carry about six people. Alternatively, a party boat costs $45 per person and carries 10-12 people. A license is required and that costs $6.75. You can buy a license at bait shops and other stores where fishing supplies are sold. The limit for salmon is two chinooks a day. The minimum size is 20 inches.

BOTTOM FISHING. This is done year round, but the best time is from January to March. The bottom fish caught in this way are usually rock fish, cabezon and ling cod. To catch halibut, the boat has to go 12-15 miles out to deeper waters. In either case, it can be very rough, so go prepared with seasick remedies.

One of my favorite ways to entertain guests – the sort who don't mind getting wet, tired or becoming redolent from handling bait – is to take them on a **crabbing** expedition. This activity, for which a license is not required, can be done in river mouths and bays all along the coast, including Washington. I can highly recommend Alsea Bay, at the town of Waldport, about 150 miles north of the California line. This is what happens on such an excursion.

We choose the best time, April through September, and in the morning we drive from Eugene to Waldport – a two-hour trip. In Waldport we proceed to **McKinley's Marina** (☎ 503-563-4656), a mile east of town on Highway 34. The marina's owner tells us which place is currently good for crabbing. Armed with this information (and perhaps some cold beer), we load ourselves into a 15-foot outboard boat, equipped with three rings (collapsible net covered pots) and a supply of bottom-fish bait. A sharp knife and heavy gloves are also important. Then we set out into the scenic, generally placid bay to the recommended spot, usually a mile or two towards the sea.

Bait fish is then tied into the rings and these are tossed into the bay, their position being marked by small buoys attached by rope to the ring. We then begin a series of circuits, pulling up a ring (they have to be pulled up rapidly or the crabs will escape) every 15 or so minutes. With three rings, this keeps all hands (gloved, of course) busy.

Usually crabs will be found in every attempt. But many of them are either too small or are females which cannot be kept. The keepers are males, no smaller than 5¾ inches wide. In time one learns how to handle crabs, so the big claws – which can be vicious – are avoided.

After three hours, which costs about $40, we have our limit if we are lucky – 12 crabs to a person.

Back at the marina, the operators, for a small fee, will clean the crabs, boil them and put them on ice. After that, we're on our way home where, with some tomatoes, mayonnaise, French bread and maybe a chilled bottle of Chablis, we eat Dungeness crabs to the point of gluttony.

MUSSELS. Sometimes called "the poor man's oyster," these gems are found clustered on rocks that are washed by the sea. To gather them, find a beach with rocks that are mostly submerged except at low tide. There are scores of such beaches along this coast. **Note:** Inquire locally to be sure there isn't a "red tide." This condition is caused by excessive amounts of microscopic flagellates that produce a potent neurotoxin. It accumulates in shellfish, making them poisonous when consumed.

Choose a day with a low tide and, armed with a hammer and heavy screwdriver, find a rock that's covered with the blue-black two- to six-inch mussels. Pry and chisel them from the rock. Each person is allowed to take 72 of them.

Soak the mussels in water with some cornmeal as quickly as possible (this flushes sand from their systems). Then scrub the "beard" from each mussel and steam them until the shells open. Discard all mussels that don't open.

Beyond that, there are a lot of options – all delicious. Eat them from the shell with a little lemon. Lace them with onions, garlic, seasoning and a little wine for a stew. Chill them for an hors d'oeuvre or include them with shrimp, clams, halibut, and crabs in a cioppino.

RAZOR CLAMS. Razor clams are gathered from beach areas exposed at low tide. Watch for a pencil-sized bubble hole in the sand. Then, using a shovel, dig toward the sea about six inches and twist the shovel to dislodge the clam. The limit is 24 clams. No license is required.

To eat them, boil in water until the shells open. Wash in cold sea water and remove the meat. Discard the gills and dark parts, slit into flat steaks, dip in egg and cracker crumbs and brown quickly in hot oil.

WHALEWATCHING. This can be done from several ports. Newport and Depoe Bay are probably the best. Ask locally if whales have been spotted and, if so, sign up for a party boat (about $35 a person). If you're fortunate, you'll encounter groups of huge gray whales migrating between the Arctic and Baja California.

North from Coos Bay

From Coos Bay, going north, U.S. 101 crosses the 150-foot-high McCullough Bridge and enters "Dune Country." For 47 miles, all the way to Florence and beyond, the road passes along ever-shifting hills of sand and a series of lakes, large and small.

The town of **Lakeside** on Ten Mile Lake, 12 miles north of Coos Bay, has good facilities. The lake itself is the scene of hiking trails and good fresh-water fishing for bass, catfish, blue gill and trout.

For folks into "dune buggy" activities, who require vehicles with flying flags, throbbing engines and pell mell assaults on dunes up to 500 feet, there are a number of possibilities. Watch for signs that advertise 25-minute dune buggy rides for $5 or U-drive buggies for $25 an hour (with a $50 deposit). Be aware, though, that in Oregon, a sharp schism exists between those who ride the buggies and those who prefer to walk and savor the peacefulness of the dunes and lakes. On occasion, the proponents of either side become extremely vocal. Clearly defined areas are maintained for both sides.

Winchester Bay

Winchester Bay, at the mouth of the Umpqua River, is a small town with a big harbor. It is one of the most productive sport and commercial fishing ports on the Oregon coast. If you find youself in this neck of the woods at the end of a day, spend the night at

Lake Marie.

Winchester Bay, rather than the town of Reedsport four miles away. If you have the time, pack a lunch and drive south on the coast access road, two miles past the Umpqua Lighthouse to Lake Marie. There is a trail (a mile or two in length) around this jewel-like lake.

A little further afield, 10 miles east of Reedsport on Highway 38 (the highway that goes inland to Eugene and Cottage Grove) at Dean's Creek, you may see groups of elk mingling with domestic cattle.

Accommodations & Dining

Places to stay in Winchester Bay are all close to the water and within walking distance of docks and restaurants. **The Winchester Bay Friendship Inn** (☎ 503-271-4871) is practically on the harbor. Moderate. If this one is full, check out the **Harbor View Motel** (☎ 503-271-3352), or **The Salmon Harbor Motel** (☎ 503-271-2732).

FOR TENT CAMPING. The Windy Cove Campground (☎ 503-271-5414), next to the harbor has 75 sites, with toilets, showers and drinking water.

FOR RV HOOK-UPS. The **Surfwood Campground** (☎ 503-271-4020) just north of Winchester has a full range of amenities. This is a popular place in the summer months and is often full.

Continuing north, Highway 101 passes through more dunes and along a series of lakes – **Tahkenitch, Siltcoos** and **Woahink.** There are camping facilities at these lakes, fishing and "dune buggy" folks will find opportunities in this area.

We enjoy a small restaurant on the harbor, the haunt of fishermen and locals, called the **Seven Seas Café** (☎ 503-271-5200). Moderately priced, they serve excellent chowder, fish and chips, and seafood platters. For more serious dining, the **Seafood Grotto** (☎ 503-271-4250) is recommended. Prices are modest.

At **Honeyman State Park** (☎ 503-997-3641), a few miles south of Florence, there's an exceptionally handsome lake – Cleawox Lake. This is an ideal choice for swimming and picnicking, but even better are the trails that wind through the dunes – a slow, sandy two-mile trek to the ocean.

Florence

Population 5,200

This town, popular for retired people, is at the mouth of the Siuslaw River and the junction of Highway 126 (the road that goes to Eugene, 65 miles to the east). Crossing the bridge northward over the Siuslaw, 101 enters "any town U.S.A." but just two blocks east is "Old Town" Florence. Here, at the river front in turn-of-the-century buildings, there's a group of trendy shops and a brace of good seafood restaurants. **Mo's**, an Oregon coast tradition, serves clam chowder – with or without shrimp – fish and chips, salmon and oysters. Prices are modest. **The Bridgewater Seafood Restaurant and Oyster Bar** tends toward fine dining – good seafood at fairly expensive prices. Away from Old Town on Highway 101 in north Florence, the **Windward Inn** offers what they call "superior coastal cuisine."

ACCOMMODATIONS. Motels in Florence are good, if not plentiful. **The Holiday Inn** (☎ 503-997-7793) and **The Château** (☎ 503-997-3481)on US 101 both have moderates rates. My favorite, for both housing and dining, is **The Pierpoint Inn** (☎ 503-997-7191) at the southern end of the bridge. The restaurant is elegant and offers views of the river and town. Rates are moderate to expensive.

SIGHTS. Five miles north of Florence – still in the dunes – watch for **Sutton Lake Campground**. Turn in to the left, park and you'll see the trailhead for one of the best walks on the coast. This is a seven-mile loop that follows parts of bubbling Sutton Creek, passes among wild rhododendrons (that bloom in spring), through canopies of weathered pine, stately spruce and quiet meadows. At **Holman Outlook**, the half-way point, there are fine views of a lonely stretch of coast.

The Sea Lion Caves, 12 miles north of Florence, come next. This attraction has been around more than 50 years. It delivers visitors down a 208-foot elevator to caves inhabited by hords of (often redolent) sea lions. The elevator costs $6, but close by (on 101 just north of the elevator) you can peer down and see the mammals for free.

Heceta Head, pronounced "Ha-seeta," with its lighthouse, is one of the most photographed places on the coast. It is a mile beyond the Sea Lion Caves. Pause in this lovely cove – complete with grills, tables, toilets and water – for a picnic and, perhaps, a stroll to the lighthouse.

Just north of Heceta, the **Carl Washburne Memorial Park**, on two miles of fine beach, has facilities for both RV's and tent campers (☎ 503-547-3416).

Yachats

Population 500

Pronounced "Yah-Hots," this town just north of Cape Perpetua lies at the mouth of the Yachats River. The inhabitants, many retired, make up a community of coastal enthusiasts – for good reason, too.

The town offers plenty of options for lovers of gourmet food. **La Serre**, specializing in shellfish dishes, has dinners in the moderate price range.

ACCOMMODATIONS. There are a number of places to stay in Yachats – all good – in the moderate to expensive range. The most attractive, with grand ocean views, is **The Adobe** (☎ 503-547-3141).

Waldport

Population 1,600

This town at the mouth of the Alsea River has a utilitarian beauty. The people who live here are more inclined to work than retirement. Waldport is mentioned earlier as a favorite crabbing area (see page 10).

ACCOMMODATIONS. There are at least 10 motels in and around town. Most are on the beach. Check out the **Alsea Manor** (☎ 503-563-1112), **Cape Cod Cottages** (☎ 503-563-2106), **Deane's Oceanside Lodge** (☎ 503-563-3321), **The Sundown Motel** (☎ 503-563-3018) – all of them on 101. Inexpensive to expensive.

FOOD. Dining here is on the informal side. Just drive along the few blocks of main street (101) and examine options. Ask locally about the small restaurant to the east of town on Highway 34.

Newport

Population 8,400

Newport is 12 miles north of Waldport and nearly in reach of Oregon's centers of population – Portland, Salem, Albany and Eugene. You'll begin to see more tourists, more activity, and more sophisticated amenities in Newport.

SIGHTS. The old town of Newport, originally a turn-of-the-century seaport lies under the graceful arches of Yaquina Bay Bridge. Here, along a resplendent bay, are a mixture of shops, working canneries, restaurants, taverns and an immense fleet of commercial fishing boats. Newport is a prime place for ocean fishing. On the other side of the bay, south of town, are an important museum and aquarium – **The Mark Hatfield Science Center** (☎ 503-867-0226; admission by donation) and the **Oregon Coast Aquarium** (☎ 503-867-3474; admission $7.35). Both places are highly informative on matters of coastal sea life.

FOOD. There are a number of small places on the harbor serving chowder as well as fish and chips. The original **Mo's** family-style restaurant is there, too. For sophisticated dining, visit the **Canyon Way Bookstore and Restaurant**. It's just up the hill from the bayfront. At the eastern edge of town, **The Embarcadero Resort and Marina** has a well-appointed, somewhat private dining room.

Just beyond Otter Crest, past the churning waters of Devils Punch Bowl State Park, 101 enters Depoe Bay, where boats – commercial, sport and whale-watching – depart from the world's smallest navigable harbor. Main Street (101) has the usual collection of souvenir shops, salt-water taffy vendors and restaurants. The favorite of locals is **The Sea Hag**. They've got almost any seafood you can think of – all of it right off the boat. The salad bar is lavish. In the bar, ask the lady in charge to "play the bottles." Using a pair of spoons, she'll play some near-recognizable tunes. Prices are a little more than modest.

The Whale Cove Inn just south of town is excellent. It's small, has startling views of the sea and some of the freshest seafood on the coast. Prices are modest. **Oceans Apart**, just north of town, is also very good. This small restaurant has fabulous views from every table and the Hawaiian hosts combine northwest seafood with a blend of Hawaiian flavors and attitudes. Moderate.

Further wandering about Newport will turn up other sources of nourishment – Italian food in nearby Nye Beach, Chinese food along 101, a Mexican restaurant or two and the usual fast food outlets.

ACCOMMODATIONS. The most dramatic place to stay in Newport is the **Embarcadero Resort and Marina** (☎ 1-800-547-4779). Almost walking distance into old town this sprawling resort, which offers condos too, has fine views of the harbor. Rates are moderate to expensive. **The Hotel** Newport (☎ 502-265-9401,) complete with a large and recommended dining room, is four miles north of town. It's on a wide beach known as a good place to gather agates. Moderate to expensive.

Eight miles north of Newport – on the coast access road (old 101) – is one of Oregon's stellar attractions, **The Inn at Otter Crest** (☎ 503-765-2111). This expansive inn of 100 rooms and suites – many with fireplaces – is on a wooded point jutting into the ocean. Services include cocktail bar, restaurant, convention facilities, tennis, heated pool and nature trails. Expensive.

There are at least nine motels in and around town. **Gracie's Landing** (☎ 503-765-2311) on the harbor is posh. Rates, which include a gourmet breakfast, are moderate to expensive. **The Holiday Surf Lodge and RV Park** (☎ 503-765-2133), north of town on the beach, is another good choice. Inexpensive to moderate. Ask if Chief Depoe, a Siletz Indian, is around. The title on his badge says, "Chief." We've always been happy there.

Other motels include **The Inn at Arch Rock** (☎ 513-765-2560), moderate; **Pirate's Cove Bed and Breakfast** (☎ 503-765-2477), expensive; **Surfrider Resort** (☎ 503-764-2311), moderate; **Troller's Lodge** (☎ 1-800-472-9335), moderate.

Gleneden

Population 800

Six to eight miles north of Depoe Bay, in Gleneden, you will find the premier hotel on the coast – perhaps in Oregon. This is the **Salishan Lodge** (☎ 503-764-2371). From what we hear it now has a well-deserved five-star rating. Don't drive past Salishan. Turn in and walk some of the grounds, golf course and all. Examine the art gallery, settle in at the dining room – ranked one of the top three restaurants in the state. If you plan to stay overnight, ask if they have any specials going. Expensive-luxury.

Lincoln City

Population 5,900

Beyond Salishan, past tidal shallows and the mouth of the Siletz River, 101 enters Lincoln City, a seven-mile-long collection of five towns. Here, you're in the realm of tourist activity from Portland, a destination with all the "schlock" imaginable, including "factory outlets," antique shops, art galleries, taverns, gift shops, indoor sports facilities, kite flying and what's known as the "shortest river in the world." Here, the D River makes a brief passage from D Lake under 101 to the ocean.

With adventure in mind, Lincoln City has little to offer. But for fun – combining the beach and city – there's a lot.

FOOD. Mo's, coastal Oregon's modestly-priced seafood institution, is at the south end of town at 51st SW 101. **The Inn at Spanish Head** in the same area has a more private dining room and a somewhat fashionable menu. **The Bay House** (5911 SW 101), with an intimate atmosphere, serves continental food. Dinner is in the expensive range. **The Dory Cove** at the north end of town is an established favorite, offering good sandwiches, seafood dishes and steaks at modest prices. **Manachi's River House**, near the D River, features Italian "gourmet" food; prices are reasonable. There's also a **Wendy's** in town, Mexican food at **Hobie's Adobe**, and Chinese fare at **Tamm's Golden Sampan**.

ACCOMMODATIONS. The list is a long one, with choices to fit any pocketbook. Driving through town, you'll see at least 45 establishments. Prices range from inexpensive to expensive. The **Inn at Spanish Head** (☎ 503-996-2161) offers sea views. Moderate to expensive. **The Dock of the Bay** (☎ 503-996-3549) on SW 51st Street offers full condominium homes at motel rates. Moderate to expensive. Also try **The City Center Motel** (☎ 503-994-2612). Inexpensive.

SIGHTS. Heading north from Lincoln City, you'll come to Highway 18, which leads to Portland, 83 miles away. The run going east crosses the wooded coast range, then enters pastoral valley lands filled with orchards and burgeoning vineyards. It passes through McMinnville – population 17,900 – site of Linfield College, near the new location of Howard Hughes' Spruce Goose. Then it goes through Newberg – population 13,000, where Herbert Hoover lived as a child – and finally enters Portland.

HIKING. Continuing up the coast road (you're now about 259 miles north of the California border), only a mile or two beyond this junction, just north of the Salmon River, you'll see a sign to **Three Rocks**. Hikers in search of extreme beauty should follow this road for 2.3 miles, then turn right for a half-mile to the trailhead of **Cascade Head**. Park here and, with packed lunch in hand, ascend through a mossy, ferned forest of spruce and hemlock, across the woods to emerge on the flanks of grassy Cascade Head, with an overview from 1,000 feet that will make you gasp.

Neskowin

This small town with a golf course, a fine beach and the **Neskowin Resort** is well worth a pause. There's the prominent wooded islet called **Proposal Rock**, referred to by the irreverent as "Proposition Rock."

Beyond Neskowin, 101 passes well inland, all the way to Tillamook, 35 miles distant. Do not stay on this road. Turn to the left at Cloverdale, eight miles north of Neskowin. This is **The Three Capes Scenic Drive**. Stop at Pacific City, where fishermen in outboard dories put off to sea through the breakers. Continue past the towns of Oceanside and Netarts to **Cape Lookout**. There is an excellent camp here, **Cape Lookout Campground** (☎ 503-842-4981), one of the best on the coast. It has 54 full RV hook-ups, tent camping, plus all services. Better yet, there's a 2½-mile trail from the park to the end of a heavily wooded, precipitous, often muddy peninsula that juts out into the sea. From a height of 830 feet, there are wonderful views of land and crashing sea.

Tillamook

Population 4,000

Tillamook, where it rains up to 72 inches a year, is home to Tillamook cheese. Courtesy of this dampness, the lush meadowed flats around the bay are the grazing grounds for happy cows that produce this renowned cheddar.

Notice the huge blimp hangars as you approach Tillamook. It was from here during WWII that blimps patrolled the Pacific Coast for Japanese submarines – sometimes successfully. Blimps are currently being built here.

Garibaldi

Population 877

Garibaldi, 12 miles north of Tillamook, is a small picturesque port – one of the better places for deep-sea fishing. The bay is good hunting ground for clams, oysters and crabs. Boats for these purposes can be rented here. You can eat at the restaurant out on the pier.

From Garibaldi, 101 hugs the coast – past Twin Rocks, Rockaway Beach with its wide stretches of peaceful sand, to a good RV/Hiker-Bike Camp, **Nehalem Bay Camp**. Nehalem offers a 7½-mile equestrian trail, as well as a bike trail. Lots of cyclists use the bike lane along 101. Notice the lightweight camping gear lashed to the sides of their bikes. These are serious long distance bikers who use the comfortably spaced campgrounds for nightly halts. One couple I know pedaled this route from Astoria to San Francisco and back – well over 1,000 miles.

Only a few miles beyond Nehalem Bay Camp, watch for **Oswald West State Park**. This is for tent camping only, but there are a couple of good walks here. One leads through rain forests of spruce and cedar on a 13-mile segment of **The Oregon Coast Trail**. The other involves a fairly arduous and steep seven-mile climb to the top of **Neahkahnie Mountain** (1,710 feet). The summit offers spectacular 360-degree views.

Cannon Beach

Population 1,200

Named for a cannon that washed ashore from a schooner in 1846, Cannon Beach is a delightful oceanfront town. It's reached by using the beach loop that leaves 101 and passes through the suburb of Tolovana Park. Beaches are good here; you can walk on them for at least six miles. In the '20s, before the coast highway was completed, motorists drove these beaches at low tide and traversed areas without beaches on rough unpaved roads, using ferries across river mouths. It was slow going. Still, it must have been high adventure.

Downtown Cannon Beach lies right on the shore. Along Hemlock, the main street that looks like a California coast town without palm trees, there's a gathering of shops, art galleries, bookstores, restaurants, cottages and "watering holes." This is a good town for strolling.

Dominating the beachfront is one of the most photographed scenes on the coast – **Haystack Rock**. At 235 feet, it's one of the tallest monoliths on earth.

ACCOMMODATIONS. At Tolovana Beach, the **Tolovana Inn** (☎ 503-436-2211) is a nicely positioned, handsome place. Moderate to expensive. Signs point the way to hotels and rental beach cabins, which are somewhat less expensive.

Cannon Beach, coupled with Tolovana Park, has at least 25 motels, ranging from inexpensive to moderate. They are easy to find.

FOOD. Park somewhere in town and wander the main street. Step into what looks good and check posted menus. Try **The Morris Fireside Restaurant**, a log building that serves moderately-priced steaks and seafood.

SIGHTS. Ecola State Beach is two miles north of Cannon Beach. It's for day-use only, but a trail setting out from there will lead hikers through a dense conifer forest to **Indian Beach**. From the beach, peer out at the **Tillamook Rock Lighthouse**, a weathered island a mile out. The light no longer operates.

The most direct route to Portland from here is via Highway 26. From near Ecola Park, the highway takes you 65 miles to Portland. It's a route that combines the forested coastal range with inland vistas of rolling hills studded with oaks, maples, vineyards and orchards.

Serious hikers will want to use the first 15 miles of this road for access to 3,283-foot **Saddle Mountain**. Turn left off Highway 26 at the sign to the trailhead, park and hike a zigzag route up about three miles to the summit. On a clear day climbers will be rewarded with views of the Columbia River as it empties into the ocean, of Mt. Hood, Mt. St. Helens, even Washington's Mt. Rainier.

Seaside

Population 5,400

This beach town, where the Necanicum River flows into the sea, is eight miles north of Cannon Beach. Seaside is pure resort. It has a two-mile boardwalk and a playground-littered beach that's wide and firm.

Historically, it's an important place. This was the end of the Lewis and Clark Trail that wound its way across the continent. It was here, in 1805-06, that the two explorers wintered and, while wintering, built a salt cairn to produce the supply of salt needed for their return trip. The salt cairn can be seen, appropriately enough, on Lewis and Clark Way in Seaside.

In more recent days, I remember Seaside as a place where high school and college students would gather. I think it was spring break, a time of license and noisy misbehavior. I recall going from Portland on the long-gone steamer, *America* ($3 round trip), then by train from Astoria to Seaside. We'd stay in cheap rooming houses for $2 or $3 a night. Some of these accommodations are still there, but they've been renovated somewhat and now cost $35-$80.

FOOD AND ENTERTAINMENT. Stroll down Broadway, get chili, clam chowder, Chinese food, hot dogs, cotton candy, beer and margaritas. Nearby, there's indoor swimming and tennis, bike rentals, video games, the lot.

ACCOMMODATIONS. There are at least 40 motels, bed-and-breakfast inns, and hotels in town. Try the **Shilo Inn Ocean Front**, ☎ 503-738-9571. Moderate to luxury. The dining room is excellent. **The Best Western Ocean View Resort** (☎ 503-738-3334) has an equally good dining room. Moderate to expensive. Lots of other motels set away from the beach are less pricey.

Gearhart

Gearhart, only a few miles north of Seaside, is a very different community. It's a quiet, substantial residential place with a new and very attractive condominium development. For golfers, there's an 18-hole public golf course.

Astoria

Population 10,000

This is the end of the line for northbound Oregon coast travelers. Beyond, over the 4.1-mile toll bridge, Washington lies waiting. But don't rush on. Pause in this non-touristed port at the mouth of the Columbia River, a town that has a legacy of canneries, logging, fishing, a steady procession of ships from all over the world and an old world Scandinavian tradition – steam baths, lutefish and all.

Why Astoria didn't outdistance San Francisco or Seattle puzzles me. Its position, with a fine harbor and the Columbia River that drains productive areas of wheat, agriculture and lumber, should have made it greater than it is.

SIGHTS. Begin by visiting the **Astoria Column**, which is 635 feet above the Columbia River. Do a walking tour of fine mansions from the 1800s along 15th and 18th Streets.

Visit the **Columbia River Maritime Museum** near the harbor. You'll see vintage fishing boats, sternwheel river boats, Indian canoes, the *Lightship Columbia*, a WWII destroyer and maps and paintings reflecting explorers that pre-date Lewis and Clark.

ACCOMMODATIONS. For a nautical environment and good dining look at the **Red Lion Inn** (☎ 503-325-7373). Moderate. **The Rosebriar Hotel** (☎ 503-325-7427) near the Maritime Museum is a pleasant place to stay. It provides a full breakfast. Expensive. There are others. The **Shilo Inn** (☎ 503-861-2181) is moderate. **Astoria Inn Bed and Breakfast** (☎ 503-325-8153), Irving Avenue, has moderate rates. The **Grandview Bed and Breakfast** (☎ 503-325-5555), Grand Avenue, is inexpensive to moderate.

FOOD. Drive down to the waterfront and try the **Pacific Rim** for pizza, the **Ship Inn** for casual seafood dining, **Little Denmark** for sandwiches and the **Red Lion Sea Fare Restaurant** for seafood. It has a cocktail bar and Sunday brunches.

Going from Astoria along Highway 30 to Portland, about 110 miles, the road follows the Columbia River. But little of the river can be seen and the trip can be done quickly.

Harking back to the days of ferryboat travel, to a taste of river life on the lower reaches of the peaceful Columbia, consider stopping at **Westport** (about 25 miles east of Astoria). Inquire here about the ferry that weaves its way across the river, around a mid-stream island and ends in Cathlamet on the Washington side. The fare is about $2.50 and the trip delightful.

From Cathlamet, continue down the Washington side to Vancouver and go across the Highway 5 Bridge into Portland.

Portland

Population 437,000
The Metropolitan Area 1,477,000

When I grew up in Portland, before the War, it was more big town than city. Seattle to the north and San Francisco to the south eclipsed Portland. We didn't mind; in fact, we preferred it that way. The Portland of those days had its colorful side. On the one hand it was staid, orderly and solid, a quiet town handsomely positioned between mountain ranges at the confluence of the Willamette and Columbia Rivers. On the other hand, there was a seamier part of town that served sailors, lumbermen, fishermen, cattlemen, "working stiffs" and occasional randy juveniles. In this part of "old Portland" – mostly the N.W. blocks – there were shabby hotels, taverns and a collection of no-nonsense two-dollar brothels. In the adjoining blocks, Chinatown provided measures of

Portland Region

Columbia River

30

St. Helens

47

26

6

Willamette River

47 Hillsboro

8

Beaverton

Tigard

99 W

PORTLAND

30 84

212

Welches 26 → Mt. Hood

Newberg

Oregon City

5 Canby

Woodburn

224

N

30 MILES

Portland

N Ainsworth St

Killingsworth St

99E

Interstate Ave

N Albania Ave

5

N Going St

N Missippi Ave

N Vancouver Ave

N Williams Ave

Martin Luther King Jr. Blvd

NE 15th Ave

N Greenley Ave

NE Fremont St

Willamette River

NW Front Ave

Yeon Ave

30

405

5

30

NW Vaughn St

Fremont Bridge

NE Hancock St

NE Broadway

NW Marshall St

NE Weilder St

84   30

NW Glisan St

NE Sandy Blvd

NW Everett

Burnside St

E Burnside St

SW 18th St

11th Ave

Park Ave

SW 2nd Ave

Front Ave

SE Stark Ave

SE Morisson St

Martin Luther King Jr. Blvd

5

SE Madison St

SE 20th Ave

SW Canyon Rd

405

26

SW Patton Rd

SE 12th Ave

Ladd Ave

SE Division St

Terwilliger Blvd

26

SE Powell Blvd

26

Dosch Dr

SE McLoughlin Blvd

SE 17th Ave

SE 26th Ave

10

Ross Island

N

5

Hardtack Island

99E

SE 28th Ave

SW Macadam Ave

SE Bypee Blvd

1 MILE

43

authentic exotica with its illegal but widely known "lottery houses," a few laundries and several good restaurants.

There were also, as I recall, three vaudeville cum burlesque theaters that featured Western movies. Erickson's Bar (no longer in existence) near the Burnside Bridge, was said to have the longest bar on the west coast, an establishment staffed by a battery of athletic bartenders. I'm told that at one time (well before my appearance) drunks were often "Shanghaied" at Erickson's and woke up the next morning on outbound ships.

Portland has changed since then and, while it's a full-grown city, much of the past is retained. The beloved, flamboyant **Rose Festival** – that rivals Pasadena's Tournament of Roses – continues. "A rose for you in Portland grows" they used to say. To which, with rain in mind, some wag responded, "A nose for you in Portland blows."

What used to be the seamy side of Portland has been gentrified and, while elements of the homeless still roam this area, fashionable restaurants have made generous use of what once was. Chinatown flourishes with good places to eat and shop. The formerly shabby waterfront along a once-polluted Willamette River (you can almost drink from it now) has grassy parks, walkways, fountains, marinas, attractive condos, good hotels and restaurants.

Portland is a user-friendly town. It's a city with good public transport, a place that lends itself to ad-lib wanderings and metropolitan adventure. I will only add the essentials and leave the adventure to you. But keep in mind that the city, divided by the Willamette River, is further split into four areas – S.W., N.W., S.E., and N.E. The city center is in S.W.-N.W. Portland.

Accommodations

Flying into Portland, you'll arrive at the International Airport in N.E. Portland, 10 miles from the city center. Fare by charter bus to nearly any city center hotel will be $8.50.

Stay, if you must, at motels and hotels near the airport. **The Sheraton Airport Hotel** (☎ 503-281-2566) is expensive. **The Courtyard Airport Hotel** (☎ 503-252-3206), **The Ramada Inn** (☎ 503-255-6511) and **The Econo Lodge** (☎ 800-4-CHOICE) are all moderate. Alternatively, you can stay in the suburbs, a little closer in, for less. There is a wide selection of motels up and down 82nd Street in N.E.-S.E. Portland or on the west side along S.W. Barbur Boulevard. At the north end of town on or near Interstate 5 along the Columbia River, there are several motels, including **The Red Lion Motor Inn** (☎ 503-283-4466) at Jantzen Beach. Moderate to expensive.

To truly appreciate Portland, however, stay downtown where options and prices are more varied. A long-time favorite of Oregonians and an institution among Portland hotels is the **Mallory Hotel** (☎ 503-223-6311). Moderate. The Mallory has an exceptionally good restaurant and is in walking distance of town. It has its own parking lot. **The Riverside Inn** (☎ 503-221-0711) on S.W. Morrison has fine views of the Willamette River and is within strolling distance from anywhere in town. Prices are moderate. Ask about corporate rates. It has its own parking lot. **The Heathman Hotel** (☎ 503-241-4100), with its elegant restaurant, is a historic institution with luxurious accommodations. It's right in the center of things on Broadway and Salmon. Expensive to luxury. **The Imperial Hotel** (☎ 503-228-7221), downtown on Broadway and Stark, is a comfortable choice. Moderate. Ask about their weekend special. **The Hilton** (☎ 503-226-1611) is in the center of town and offers predictably good amenities. Expensive to luxury. **The Benson** (☎ 503-228-2000), on Broadway and Oak, has been around for years. An opulent choice, moderate to luxury. **The Mark Spencer** (☎ 503-224-3293), 409 S.W. 11th – around the corner from "Jakes," one of Portland's best restaurants – is a modestly priced, excellent choice. Ask about special rates.

Dining

One of my favorites – and I'm joined by many – is a Portland landmark, **Jakes Famous Crawfish** at 401 S.W. 12th. Sit for awhile in the congenial and often-crowded front bar, then adjourn to a dining room filled with artwork, where you will be served a wide range of seafood. Jakes is on the expensive side, but well worth it. **The London Grill** in the Benson Hotel, another Portland landmark, serves continental cuisine and has an extensive wine list. Moderate to expensive.

For Japanese food, reserve a private room at **The Bushgarden** on 900 S.W. Morrison. Remove your shoes and settle down, à la Japan, to be served an elegant sukiyaki with tempura shrimp. Prices are reasonable.

In **Chinatown**, just across Burnside from the center of town, there are several very good Chinese restaurants. You can hardly go wrong.

For Italian dining, among the best in Portland, right downtown on 3rd and Morrison, step into **Alessandros. The Atwater Restaurant and Lounge** on the 30th floor of the U.S. Bancorp Tower, 111 S.W. 5th Avenue, has a fine view and excellent American cuisine. Expensive.

Dan and Louis Oyster Bar, near the river on 208 S.W. Ankeny Street, goes back at least 75 years. Portlanders revere this place. Even if you don't like oysters, plenty of options remain – crab, shrimp, clams, stews, salads, salmon. Inexpensive to moderate.

For continental food, **L'Auberge**, 2601 N.W. Vaughn – close but not walking distance from downtown – has dignified, excellent dining at moderate to expensive rates. **McCormick and Schmick's Seafood Restaurant**, on 235 S.W. 1st Avenue, has live music, a bar and (in addition to good seafood) fine continental dining. Expensive.

Dining options are far more extensive than listed here. They are all over town – French, German, Italian, Chinese, Mexican – and can be found in hotel room brochures.

Getting Around

The best way to see downtown is by walking. Start at the **Tom McCall Waterfront Park**, a beautiful two-mile promenade. In the same area at Riverside Place ask about the sternwheeler, *Rose*, which goes up and down the lovely Williamette River.

From the waterfront walk, take a **bus** or **MAX Light Rail Mass Transit** (free in downtown areas) to the historic **Old Town District**. Step into **Powell's City of Books** on Burnside, one of America's largest bookstores. See **Pioneer Courthouse Square** with its coffee house and fountain on S.W. Yamhill.

Visit the **Portland Art Museum** and **The Oregon Historical Society** in the leafy park blocks. Take in an opera, symphony or ballet at **The Portland Center for the Performing Arts**. If it's Saturday, stroll to 108 W. Burnside and the **Saturday Market**, where you can buy arts and crafts, see street performances and eat from a variety of inexpensive stalls.

Take the **Tri Met Bus Line** from 5th and Washington to **Washington Park** in the hills west of town. Near there, you will find the **Zoo**, the **Hoyt Arboretum**, historic **Pittock Mansion**, and the **Japanese Gardens**. For hiking, check out the 14-mile **Wildwood Trail**, which is within eye-shot of downtown Portland. The trail, a bit of wilderness surrounded by city, starts from near the Zoo on Canyon Road.

Across town on the east side of the Willamette River Walk is **Laurelhurst Park**, off S.E. 39th Street. See **Mt. Tabor** with its extinct crater in S.E. Portland. In N.E., take a trip to the **Grotto** near N.E. 82nd Street. Visit the **Rhododendron Gardens** – 62 acres of inspiring gardens near Reed College in S.E. Portland.

For the rail journey across town and beyond to suburban Gresham, take the 45-minute **MAX** run – $2.40 round trip.

Don't rush out of Portland, it will grow on you. But when it's time to leave, you're in a good position to move up the Columbia River to the east into the Gorge and on to Mt. Hood.

Mt. Hood & the Columbia River Gorge

Within the roughly 81 miles between Portland and the town called The Dalles, nature's grandeur is unusual, a condensation of sheer cliffs, a majestic river, dozens of waterfalls and hiking trails into spectacular wilderness areas.

To get at this beauty there are two approaches. The direct route running east from Portland along I-84 will deliver you at river level to The Dalles. Traveling this freeway you can make most of the important stops at parks, trails, waterfalls, or windsurfing spots, in addition to finding lodging and meals.

But to really experience the Gorge, take exit 17 at Troutdale and use the "scenic route," a slow, winding panoramic run built in 1915. **The Crown Point Vista House**, built in 1916, is the first attraction. Views of the river from this historic 730-foot perch are excellent. Coming up next, after only a few miles, are **Latourell Falls, Wahkeena** and **Bridal Veil Falls**.

Mt. Hood & the
Columbia River Gorge

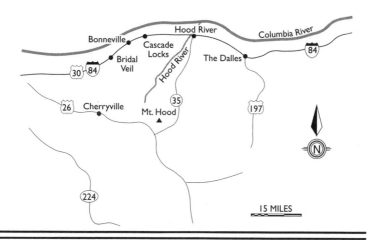

Spectacular **Multnomah Falls** follows, a 620-foot cataract tumbling from a rocky cliff. This is a fine destination, a photographer's dream with a park at the bottom ideal for picnicking. Hikers should note that from Multnomah Falls there is a dramatic trail, **The Multnomah-Wahkeena Falls Loop**. This is a 3½-mile loop trek that climbs 1,000 feet in elevation, then descends past Wahkeena Falls to the Multnomah Falls Lodge. Views on this trail are breathtaking.

Just beyond Multnomah are another pair of falls, **Oneonta** and **Horsetail**. There is a gentler hike here, a two-mile round trip that gains 400 feet in elevation. This trail begins at the parking area of Horsetail Falls and uses switchbacks to reach the top of Upper Horsetail. It then passes

Oneonta Gorge.

above Oneonta Falls and returns to the road less than a mile from where you started.

Continuing east only a few miles to Dodson, the old road rejoins I-84 and moves on to **Bonneville Dam**. Built in the 30's, this dam is a valuable hydroelectric source to the northwest. You can tour the dam if you like, or you can pause and watch boats and barges pass through the gates. From a glass-enclosed underwater center you can see salmon going upstream to spawn.

About three miles east of Bonneville, past the **Bridge of the Gods** (a bridge spanning the Oregon/Washington border where, according to regional history and Indian lore, there was once a natural bridge), I-84 enters **Cascade Locks**. This now-peaceful little town used to be a bustling community when Bonneville Dam was being constructed in the 30's. It even hummed a little before the turn of the century when shipping locks were built to allow the passage of steamboats around the vicious rapids.

For a taste of those steamboat days, check out the sternwheeler, *Columbia Gorge*, that sails during the summer. This two-hour narrated cruise departs from Cascade Locks Marine Park. The fare is $10.95 (☎ 503-223-3928).

ACCOMMODATIONS. An inexpensive place to stay in Cascade Locks is **The Scandian Motor Lodge** (☎ 503-374-8417). It has restaurants nearby.

Eagle Creek, in the same area, is a worthwhile destination for hikers and campers. At the **Eagle Creek Campground** there are sites for tents and RV's with tables, grills, toilets and firewood. The user's fee is $5.

HIKING. For hiking, Eagle Creek has one of the most beautiful trails in the Gorge. Here you can do a rigorous 13-mile, one-way trek to **Wahtum Lake**. There are campsites along this trail, one at four miles, without a shelter, and one with a shelter at 7.5 miles. Do selected bits of this trail if you prefer. For example, take trail 440 from eagle Creek Camp to **Punchbowl Falls**, a four-mile round trip.

The Pacific Crest Trail. For the granddaddy of all trails (in Washington, Oregon and California), continue through Cascade Locks and take the road marked "Airport-Industrial Park." Go about two miles and watch for the sign saying **"Pacific Crest Trailhead."** This trail, beginning at the Canadian border in Washington state, runs through Washington, Oregon and California, all the way to Mexico. I've got friends who have done the entire Oregon portion of the trail – but not in one go. They've walked parts of it one summer, continued the following summer, and in due time traveled the dramatic spine of Oregon to the California border. In high summer you can walk selected parts of the trail with ease. More of this trail on page 64.

Hood River

Population 4,600

East of Eagle Creek, the Columbia River widens and the enclosing mountains begin to show patches bare of trees, a sign of the approaching desert. Hood River appears at this point, a major apple and pear growing community in the shadow of Mt. Hood to the west. It is a place of beauty.

The brisk wind that blows down the Gorge at Hood River makes this area the "Sail Boarding Capital of the World." To try it yourself, take exit 64 off I-84 and go to the **Columbia Gorge Sailpark at Port Marina Park**. Here they give windsurfing lessons and rent equipment.

ACCOMMODATIONS. Spend an elegant night at the **Columbia Gorge Hotel** (☎ 503-386-5566). Built in the 1920's, this beautifully restored building overlooks the Columbia and is on very attractive grounds. The dining room is superb. Rates are on the expensive side. Ask about special rates.

Whether you're a windsurfer, skier or golfer, **The Hood River Inn** (☎ 503-386-2200) is excellent, at moderate rates. **The Vagabond Lodge** (☎ 503-386-2992) overlooks the river and is close to a nearby restaurant. Inexpensive to moderate.

DINING. For dining in style, pricey style, the **Columbia Gorge Hotel** is hard to beat. Food is continental. **The Stonehenge Inn**, in an old restored house, provides country-style American food. Moderate. **The Hood River Inn** has a riverside grill and a comfortable lounge. Rates are modest.

Mt. Hood

Elevation 11,239 feet

For years Oregonians have been astounding out-of-state friends by taking them on the **Mt. Hood Loop** trip. Sometimes this run is done in one day, a trip beginning and ending in Portland. A one-day venture of four to six hours is happily possible but several days are better. For example, having negotiated the Columbia Gorge to Hood River, take Highway 35 south under the looming Mt. Hood to the junction of west-bound Highway 26 – about 35 miles. After a few miles on Highway 26, watch for the turnoff to **Timberline Lodge**, which is about eight miles up the flank of Mt. Hood. Timberline Lodge (☎ 503-272-3311), a stone and timber castle built by the Works Progress Administration in the 30's, is a national landmark. It sits where the trees end at 6,000 feet. Rates are moderate to expensive. Food in the dining room is at award-winning levels and cocktail time in the Blue Ox Bar will take the chill off a day of skiing or climbing.

HIKING AND CLIMBING. Climbing Mt. Hood, the highest peak in Oregon, should be done with the utmost care. But, with good equipment and at the right time of the year, nearly all reasonably fit people can make the ascent.

From May to July are the best months; a very early morning start (when the snow is still firm) is the best time of day. Count on the trip up and back from Timberline Lodge to be a good 12 hours. If you're not experienced, go with a guided group and choose the easiest way – in this case the Hogback route.

More experienced climbers will want to go via such approaches as the Mazama, Wyeast and Castle Crag routes. Bear in mind that, while thousands of climbers have made the climb, others have been tragically unsuccessful. This mountain demands respect.

For shorter, less demanding treks on the mountain, ask at the lodge about other hikes. There are lots of them, including a trail all the way around the mountain.

From Timberline, return to Highway 26 and go west via Government Camp, a ski resort, downhill through dense forests of fir all the way to Portland.

CAMPING. Along this way there are good campsites. **Camp Creek**, about eight miles downhill from Government Camp, is on a delightful babbling creek, close to good hiking trails. There are 24 units at Camp Creek. The user's fee is $5-$10. Near the tiny town of Rhododendron, where gas and restaurants are available, **Toll Gate Campground** has RV sites, water, toilets, nature trails and fair trout fishing. In rapid succession, Welches with its golf course appears, Wemme comes up with a good restaurant, **The Inn Between**, and then the towns of Sandy and Gresham and, finally, Portland reappears.

Southern Oregon

Coming from California, the most direct route into Oregon is along I-5, the freeway which runs from the Mexican border all the way to Canada. Entering Oregon, this road crosses the 4,310-foot Siskiyou Summit, a scenic drive. But, if you do it in winter, check weather conditions first. Snow devices are sometimes required and high winds can make RV-trailer travel iffy.

Skiers should note that, from Siskiyou Summit, there is a road going west five miles that leads to **Mt. Ashland**. Here, a chairlift ascends 1,180 feet to the top of the mountain. From there, skiers can choose a number of runs to the bottom. In the summer, there are good hiking trails in the same area.

Ashland

Population 16,200

Ashland, about 15 miles north of the California border, may be Oregon's most enchanting town. It's a place proudly filled with remnants of the past – Victorian houses, pioneer vintage buildings, art galleries, antique shops, bed-and-breakfast inns by the score, a university and a rambling green park, Lithia, with its "therapeutic" mineral water.

More importantly, Ashland has its theatrical side. Plays of all kinds are performed here, but the most important attraction is the **Oregon Shakespeare Festival**. From mid-February through October, it presents 11 plays. Appropriate to Shakespeare, these plays are

Southern Oregon

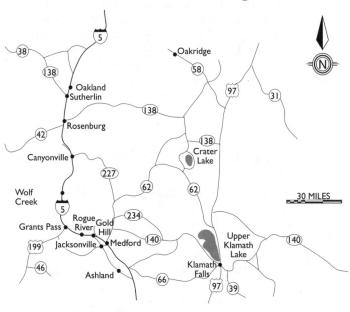

done on an outdoor Elizabethan stage and in two indoor theaters. For information and tickets, ☎ 503-482-4331.

ACCOMMODATIONS. By rough count I come up with at least 28 places to stay in Ashland. They're easily seen and their rates fall between inexpensive and luxury. For starters, here are a few. **The Stratford Inn,** ☎ 503-488-2151, five blocks from the Shakespeare theaters, is very pleasant and rates are moderate. **The Chanticleer Inn,** ☎ 503-482-1919, on Clay Street, is a comfortable selection. Moderate to expensive. **The Country Willows,** ☎ 503-488-1590, another bed-and-breakfast inn on Clay Street, has vintage farmhouse charm. Moderate to expensive. **The Regency Inn,** ☎ 503-482-4700, near the Shakespeare theaters, is a comfortable motel with inexpensive rates.

FOOD. Anything and everything is possible here. You'll need little help. But for something truly reflecting Ashland, consider the following. For French cuisine, visit **Chateaulin** on Main Street – expensive for dinner. For American food, step into **Omar's Fresh**

Fish and Steaks on Siskiyou Street – moderate. Fine continental meals are served at **Primavera** on Hagardine. Moderate.

When you're not taking in a play or "doing Shakespeare," take a healing walk in the 90-acre, leafy green **Lithia Park**. Or, for year-round wine tasting, check out **The Ashland Vineyards and Winery**. This is two miles off I-5 at exit 14.

Jacksonville

Population 1,900

North of Ashland, about eight miles, leave I-5 and take Highway 99 west through the orchards to the old Gold Rush town of Jacksonville. In this town there's a collection of at least 80 preserved pioneer buildings and museums that reflect pioneer life in the 1800's. Do a walking tour of these attractions, then top it off with a meal in a local café or a fine meal at the more pricey **Jacksonville Inn Dinner House**.

Wine buffs may want to drive eight miles south of town on SR 238 to the **Valley View Vineyard** for tours and tasting.

Medford

Population 47,000

Medford, about seven miles from Jacksonville, is an attractively utilitarian "mini city," a commercial center for agriculture, manufacturing and lumber. Fruit growing in the surrounding area is important to the region and Medford is home to the widely known **Harry and David's Oregon Country Store** (2836 S. Pacific Road). Here you can order, buy, or have shipped, a wide selection of dried fruit.

People who live and work in Medford are not only enthusiastic about their well honed amenities but about what nature provides in their vicinity – for example, the road that runs northeast through raw natural beauty, 76 miles to **Crater Lake**. We'll get to Crater Lake under Central Oregon.

ACCOMMODATIONS. *Where to Stay in Oregon* lists about 17 motels and inns. This can be obtained from the Oregon Visitor's Association, Box 1, 26 S.W. Salmon St., Portland OR 97201. Coming up I-5 watch for the motels. **The Best Western,** ☎ 503-773-8266, on Riverside Drive has moderate rates. **The Pear Tree Motel,** ☎ 503-535-4445, off I-5 at exit 24, also has moderate rates.

Please note that "exit numbers" refer roughly to the miles from the California border.

FOOD. There are plenty of choices, but for casual elegance try **Misty's** at the Red Lion Inn on Riverside Drive. Moderate. **Stanley's Restaurant and Lounge** has simple but hearty food – smoked ribs, burgers. Moderate. Create your own pizzas at the **Golden Spike** on Riverside Drive. For Mexican food try **Loli's** on Front Street. Moderately priced.

Gold Hill

Population 17,500

This small town just north of Medford is advertised as the place where gravity plays strange tricks. Examine their claims by visiting **The Oregon Vortex**, where the usual laws of physics don't apply, $4-$6.

From Gold Hill on to Grants Pass, 25 or so miles, I-5 follows the Rogue River.

Grants Pass

Population 17,500

Because of its location, Grants Pass is an ideal base for a number of activities – some of the best Oregon has to offer.

To begin with, Grants Pass is located on an important junction. This is where the Redwood Highway (Highway 199), coming from California 60 miles to the southwest, joins I-5. For travelers not taking the coast road north (Highway 101,) the Redwood Highway will deliver them to Grants Pass via the following route.

SIGHTS. Cave Junction, population 1,100 with a scattering of easily found motels and restaurants, is about 14 miles north of the border. More importantly, it's here that a winding road, SR 46, runs east into the wooded Siskiyou Mts. about 20 miles to **The Oregon**

Caves National Monument. Towing a trailer on this road is not advised, and travel in winter can be difficult for any vehicle.

The Oregon Caves, at an altitude of 4,000 feet, are classified as "remote" and are visited with a little worthwhile effort.

The caves, complete with stalactites, stalagmites, pillars and canopies of calcite, have a dramatic series of connected passages and chambers. One of them, Paradise Lost, a room 60-feet high, has a series of water-formed decorations that resemble a petrified waterfall.

Touring the cave, in stout walking shoes, is reasonably strenous and involves continual stooping to negotiate narrow passages. Wear warm clothing, as the cave's temperature is always at 41°F. The tour lasts 75 minutes. Admission: $6.75 for adults, $3.75 for children.

This is true wilderness, a remote area with raw beauty that includes one of the earth's rarest shrubs, the Kalmiopsis Leachiana. The shrub looks like a small rhododendron.

Hikers into this unforgiving area should be well prepared. Potable water is scarce, poison oak and ticks are widespread and rattlesnakes are native to the area. One other matter may be of importance. It is said that some of the locals grow marijuana and are suspicious of strangers. When approaching a dwelling, make yourself heard. Do not creep up on anyone.

RAFTING. The Illinois is more challenging than the nearby Rogue. Check with the river-running organizations, someone like **Wild Water Adventures**, P.O. Box 249, Creswell, OR 97426; ☎ 503-895-4465. Or **Oregon River Experiences**, 2 Jefferson Parkway, #D7, Lake Oswego, OR 97035; ☎ 800-827-1358.

From Selma to Grants Pass is about 21 miles and, with further adventure in mind, Grants Pass is a good base for operations.

ACCOMMODATIONS. There are 25-30 easily found motels in town ranging from inexpensive to expensive. But I've always enjoyed being right on the river, in town at **The Riverside Inn**, ☎ 503-476-6873. Moderate.

There are good accommodations near the caves, such as **The Oregon Caves Chateau**. This admirable lodge, of historic registry, is on scenic grounds. It has an inviting lobby with a double fireplace, a brook running through the dining area and comfortable rooms. The lodge is open from May 9 to September 9. Rates are moderate and I'm told that a free tour of a cave comes with the price of the room.

DINING. The Riverside Inn and the **Best Western** both have pleasant cocktail lounges and popular restaurants. **The Yankee Pot Roast**, in a historic house, has American food at moderate rates.

The Rogue River

This 100-mile river, born in the high country near Crater Lake, gathers its tributaries from mountain streams and loops its way through Grants Pass, then through the Siskiyou Mountains to the coast at Gold Beach.

RAFTING. For those who want to navigate part of this exuberant river on their own, the portion from Grants Pass to Graves Creek, about 28 miles (near a road all the way), can be done without a permit. But because the river below Graves Creek, the "wild and scenic" part, is heavily used by rafters, permits are required. Permits are often hard for private rafters to get. However, licensed guides are given a preference, so it may be less hassle to sign up with one of them. A complete list of these licensed guides is available in Grants Pass, but also note the two organizations listed on page 39 in the section on rafting the Illinois River.

Assume it is summer, you have a guide with a raft and you are poised to set off from Graves Creek to negotiate the Rogue to Illahe. The distance is about 40 miles and it will take about four days. Fares for this trip will be about $500 per person (perhaps half that if a guide has last-minute spaces to fill). This fee will include professional rafting equipment, life jackets, waterproof bags for personal gear, prepared meals (generally excellent, occasionally including wine and trout if you caught it) and transportation to and from designated meeting places. You are expected to bring sleeping bags, maybe a tent and appropriate clothes.

As you move down the river, through mantles of Douglas fir, spruce, oaks and madrones, there are peaceful stretches and challenging reaches of whitewater that will get your attention. There will be vertical-walled canyons, boulder-filled mazes and abrupt drop-offs that require skill. Then, too, there will be places for drift swimming, fishing and peaceful spots to camp. This is a trip you will long remember.

HIKING. This is an alternative to rafting. Some folks prefer it because it can be done independently. It is certainly cheaper. I've done the trip both ways. Last time, equipped with appropriate tracking gear, a map and a suitable supply of Scotch, we left our car at Graves Creek and set forth. About two miles past Raine Falls, where the Rogue drops 12 feet (here rafts, without passengers, are passed down with lines), it began to rain. We trudged on, wet and ill-tempered, five miles to Big Slide Camp. The Scotch helped.

A word about this trail. There are said to be rattlesnakes along the way, although we didn't see any. There is poison oak. Water from tributary streams is said to bear traces of arsenic, but we drank the water with no ill effects. There was little climbing on this trek. We simply followed the winding river one beautiful mile after another. Fortunately, the rain stopped after the first day and the following days such campsites as Black Bear, Winkle Bar, Tucker Flat, and Blossom Bar came and went. We made around 10 miles per day. Arrival at Illahe coincided with the last of the Scotch.

However, there was a nagging fear, a worry that when we arrived at Illahe – where a marginal, lonesome road loops to the north back to Graves Creek – there would be no one to take us back. But luck was with us. Along came perhaps the only car that day, an agreeable couple who crowded us into their van for the return trip. Don't take such chances. Do a shuttle run, or arrange for someone to meet you.

Wolf Creek

From Graves Creek back to I-5, about 10 miles, the road passes through this tiny village. In the center of town there is an old stagecoach inn that dates back to the 1870's. It's been carefully restored. The food here is good and so is the sense of history.

The Safari Wildlife Game Park

Moving north up I-5 about 30 pretty miles, a turnoff to the west at exit 119 to Highway 42 leads five miles to the Game Park. This is a 600-acre preserve where exotic animals roam free. From the comfort and safety of your car, you wander among elephants, lions, tigers, cheetahs, camels, hippos, rhinos and birds of all kind. Except for the climate and vegetation, you could be in Kenya or Tanzania. Admission: $9.95 (plus $1 per car); senior citizens, $8.50; and children, $6.50.

Roseburg

Population 17,000

SIGHTS. Roseburg, known for its timber industries, has retained a turn-of-the century mystique. The best concentration of old buildings is near the city's center in the Mill-Pine District. A repository of the past, **The Douglas County Museum**, off I-5 at exit 123, has more than 15,000 photographs and artifacts relating to earlier days. It's open Tuesday through Saturday from 10 to 4. Entry is by donation.

Six wineries are located in and around Roseburg. Check out **Hillcrest Vineyard**, off I-5, at exit 123.

With adventure, beauty and unusual accommodations, SR 138 goes east out of Roseburg. It is a scenic 103-mile route that follows the Umpqua to Diamond Lake and beyond to Crater Lake. More on these two lakes later, but first we should mention the **Steamboat Inn** (☎ 503-498-2411), about 40 miles east of Roseburg. Right on the Umpqua, it is a delightful place to stay, with fine cooks and pleasant hosts. It's an ideal base for fishing, romancing and walking local trails. The rates are moderate to expensive.

RAFTING. Using Roseburg, or better yet the Steamboat Inn, as a base, the North Umpqua River, with Class III and IV rapids, offers fast-paced excitement. Try a two-day trip on this picturesque river. In Roseburg, ask about guides or check out the ones given earlier. Fees will be in the $200 range.

ACCOMMODATIONS. The Roseburg Travelodge (☎ 503-672-4836), at moderate rates, is off I-5 at exit 124. **The Shady Oaks** (☎ 503-672-2608), at exit 120, is inexpensive. **The Windmill Inn** (☎ 503-673-0901), at exit 125, has moderate rates. There are others on either side of I-5.

FOOD. The Windmill Inn has a pleasant dining room and cocktail lounge. It is moderately priced. I have always enjoyed the **Wagon**

Wheel, with easy access off I-5 at exit 125. It has good prime ribs, steaks, and seafood at moderate prices.

Oakland

Population: maybe 1,000

Not to be confused with the California city of the same name, this little town has a genuine connection with the past. The whole town looks as if it belongs in the 19th century.

To get there from Roseburg, continue up I-5 to exit 138 and proceed east a couple of miles to this startling, compact, old-world town. As on a pilgrimage, I go there from Eugene (about 50 miles to the north) on special occasions, a birthday, an anniversary or to entertain out-of-towners. Sometimes we begin activities in Oakland by stepping into a saloon at the near end of town, a place where you get hard-boiled eggs and pickled prawns from containers on the counter. We have a beer and enjoy a measure of local companionship. Then, for the pièce de résistance, we cross the street and enter **Tolly's**. This is a nostalgic, small-town restaurant with attached shop and art gallery. The ham-and-cheese sandwiches, hamburgers, Reubens and gigantic milk shakes are superb.

Moving north up I-5, the town of Sutherland appears. This is 136 miles north of the California border. From here, a turn to the west on 138, then 38, offers one of the prettiest ways to the coast, much of it along peaceful stretches of the lower Umpqua.

The Willamette Valley

Around Cottage Grove, 174 miles into Oregon, the Willamette Valley begins. This is where two branches of the Willamette approach each other, finally meeting with the McKenzie River near Eugene.

If Oregon has a vascular system and a heart, this is where it begins. This is where it forms a valley up to 40 miles wide that runs all the way north to Portland, about 127 miles.

Willamette Valley

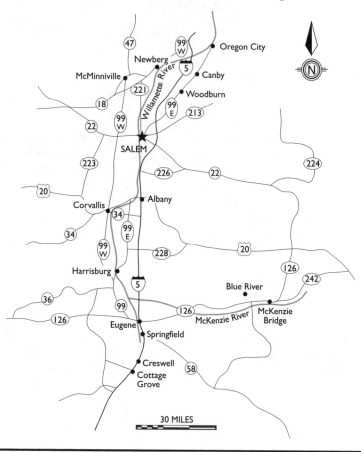

47

99 W

Newberg   Oregon City

McMinnville   Canby   5

221   Willamette River   Woodburn

18   99 E   213

22   99 W

SALEM

223   226   22   224

20

Corvallis   Albany

34

34   99 E

99 W   228   20

Harrisburg   5

126

36   Blue River   242

99   McKenzie Bridge

126   126   McKenzie River   McKenzie Bridge

Eugene   Springfield

Creswell

Cottage Grove   58

30 MILES

Cottage Grove

Population 7,400

If evening coincides with your arrival at Cottage Grove, a particularly fine stop comes to mind – **The Village Green Resort Hotel** (☎ 503-942-2491). The hotel has an elegant dining room called the Cascadia Room. Set on 16 garden-like acres, complete with golf course and jogging trails, the Village Green is a good jumping-off place for what this area has to offer. You'll see this hotel from I-5 (take exit 174). The rates are moderate.

Spend a day in and around Cottage Grove. Have a picnic at **Dorena Lake,** east of town. Examine items from pioneer mining days, circa the 1860's, at the **Cottage Grove Historical Museum**. To get deeper into the past, negotiate the winding, narrow road to the east, a 70-mile loop among weathered remains of the Bohemia Mines, where gold was discovered in 1858.

Beyond Cottage Grove, 22 miles up I-5, Oregon's second city, Eugene, and its neighbor, Springfield, come next.

Eugene

Population 112,700

I can't think of many cities that have taken better advantage of what nature has to offer, combining that with a rich cultural life. And few cities do a better job of feeding and entertaining visitors. This is also true of Eugene's neighbor, Springfield, with its 41,000 people.

Sights

To begin with, the **University of Oregon**, founded in 1876, occupies 250 beautifully groomed acres. The University, which is strong in liberal arts, has about 20,000 students. Some of these students, as on many other colleges, live a counterculture lifestyle. You may recognize the campus if you saw the movie *Animal House*, as parts of the movie were filmed here.

Wandering Oregon's leafy green campus among stately old buildings produces its own rewards. Step into the **Art Museum**, which displays Oriental artifacts, some fine Rodins, paintings and traveling exhibits. The museum is free of charge. Enter the **Library** and you will find a wide assortment of books on nearly every subject. Attend evening concerts at **Beal Hall** or watch sports activities at **Mac Court**.

Eugene is very proud of its cultural attractions. **The Hult Center for the Performing Arts** offers symphonies, ballets and opera in a series of halls that are the envy of cities three times as big.

There's other culture too, although not appreciated by everyone. The Grateful Dead have appeared in Eugene, usually at the Autzen Football Stadium. Their followers, "deadheads" from all over the country, are there too. For the few days of their presence, all Eugene hotels and motels are filled.

For contemporary art, local as well as national, visit **The Maude Kerna Art Center** near the campus.

The people who live in Eugene are a mixed lot. Many of them are associated with the university and others are in the lumber business. Some are in light industry, insurance, service-type jobs and the railroad. Many are retired and say they wouldn't live anywhere else. Other than the wet winters, which sometimes lay a pall on the soul, I strongly agree. And spring, when it happens, is always vibrant.

Fortunately, at least by California standards, real estate in Eugene is affordable. Comfortable condos are in the $90-$125,000 range. Attractive homes on wooded lots, often with a view, go for $90-$300,000. This probably won't last.

Important, too, for both residents and visitors, are the miles of jogging, biking, and walking paths that Eugene and Springfield provide. There are paths, connected by footbridges, along both sides of the Willamette River. They pass through parks, woods, rose gardens and run near shopping centers.

For river walking, park your car at **Alton Baker Park**, across the Ferry Street Bridge, and choose a loop walk, anywhere from two to eight miles.

For visual beauty, good walking too, visit **Hendricks Park** on Summit Drive near town. This park, best in May and June, is alive with rhododendrons and azaleas in the summer.

MOUNT PISGAH. Hikers, picnickers and folks who appreciate well-run arboretums should visit Mt. Pisgah in the **Buford Recreation Area**. To get there, follow 30th Avenue out of town and take Seavey Loop Road. You'll see signs at this point.

There are several options at this park. First, climb Mt. Pisgah, altitude 1,500 feet, a reasonably vigorous 1½-mile hike. Views from the top are rewarding, including, if the weather is clear, the snow-capped Three Sisters. Second, walk the wooded paths along the coastal fork of the Willamette River. Third, do one of several loop walks along the flanks of Mt. Pisgah through a well-marked arboretum.

SPENCER'S BUTTE. You'll see this butte from nearly anywhere in town. From the park at its base, found by going south on Willamette Street, there are several steep trails ascending through old growth Douglas firs to the top at 2,000 feet. The ascent will take about 45 minutes. The view is excellent, but in summer rattlesnakes are found here. Be careful of poison oak as well.

THE RIDGELINE TRAIL. In the Spencer's Butte area, reached by Fox Hollow Road, there are a series of easy trails that cover several wooded miles. In spite of the thick forest, there are occasional views of the city below.

Accommodations

Starting with premier accommodations, **The Valley River Inn** (☎ 503-687-5201), on the river near the shopping center, is well placed for shopping, dining and river footpath walking. Rates are expensive. The popular **Hilton Hotel** (☎ 503-342-2000), on 6th Avenue, is within walking distance of all downtown. Rates are moderate to expensive.

On Franklin Avenue near the university there are other fine choices. **The Angus Inn** (☎ 503-342-1293), complete with steakhouse, has moderate rates. **The Best Western Green Tree Inn** (☎ 503-485-2727) has an exceptionally fine restaurant and sometimes offers entertainment. Their rates are moderate. **The New Oregon Motel** (☎ 503-683-3669), in the same area, is popular and the rates are moderate. Drive slowly along Franklin Avenue and watch for other possible places to stay. For less expensive accommodations, drive west along 6th Street and consider such possibilities as **The Budget Host Motor Inn** (☎ 503-342-7273).

Dining

Eugene is well stocked with good places to eat. Best thing is to examine the yellow pages. You'll find that there are good milkshakes and hamburgers at **Jaime's**, on Hilyard and on Chambers.

Or you can settle down in style at **Sweetwaters** in the Valley River Inn, where they have continental and northwest cuisine at moderately expensive prices. You might also consider the Hilton, which has fine dining; moderately expensive. **The Red Lion** on Coburg Road offers a continental menu; moderately expensive. **Shojis** on Willamette Street does Hibachi-style, Japanese cooking at modest prices. **Mekalas** on 5th Avenue serves elegant Thai food at modest prices. **Mazzis** on Amazon Street serves Italian food, also at modest prices. Be sure to try their cioppino. Near the university, **The Excelsior** has a warm, unique atmosphere. It features European cuisine and is fairly expensive. Near the Hilton, **The Oregon Electric Station** is in the old depot, and some parts of it are in vintage dining cars. They specialize in steaks, seafood and salads; moderately priced. **The North Bank** on Club Road, right on the river, serves pasta, steaks, seafood and wonderful salads. It is moderately priced.

Add to all the above 16 Chinese restaurants, 16 Mexican, six Italian, two pancake houses, four vegetarian restaurants and a host of fast-food cafés. You'll have no trouble with food in Eugene.

Outside Eugene

THE MCKENZIE RIVER AND ENVIRONS. This is another area that I show with pride to out-of-state people. It's along this gem of a river that I take friends for a day or more of fishing, hiking, rafting, or simple sightseeing. I take them up the McKenzie River on Highway 126, the road that runs across the Cascade Mountains to Bend, 125 miles east of Eugene.

To get on 126, leave the northbound lane of 105 in Eugene to Highway 126. Follow signs indicating the McKenzie Highway and keep going (past Springfield) to the east. **Hendrick's Bridge Wayside** (about 14 miles from Eugene) is a good first stop. Here the McKenzie River is docile. Swimming is good (but cold). For leisurely, peaceful rafting, with only a few minor riffles, the drift to **Armitage State Park**, near Eugene, will take about five hours. Walterville is just beyond Hendricks, and from there Highway 126 weaves through pastoral land. Hazelnuts and other crops are grown here. Those who live along this river (farmers, retired folks and people who commute into Eugene) form a tightly knit but widely separated community.

Leaburg Dam, where Eugene gets some of its power, comes next and with it a pristine lake. **Goodpasture Bridge** appears a couple

McKenzie River.

of miles later. This often-photographed covered bridge crosses the McKenzie, and the road will lead visitors to an inn that deserves mention. It is the **Wayfarer Resort** (☎ 503-896-3613). Visitors here are well away from city noises. They're right on the McKenzie, next to a bubbling creek, housed in self-contained cottages. Trout fishing is close at hand and so is tennis. Moderate.

Beyond Vida, near the bridge, the character of the McKenzie changes. Now it's a fast-flowing, clear, tumultuous stream that winds between wooded hills and rows of native rhododendrons.

Keep going upriver, but if fishing is important, give thought to a pause in this area – perhaps on the Blue River. As a birthday present, I was once given a day of trout fishing on the McKenzie, along with a boat and a guide. For this purpose, we drove to the Blue River (on the McKenzie about 14 miles upriver) from Vida. There, in the early morning, we set out with a guide in one of the 16-foot drift boats that are unique to the McKenzie. We then drifted down through modest rapids and magnificent scenery to a spot near Vida, where we built a fire and cooked our morning limit. In the afternoon we caught yet another limit, which was iced and packed for later.

Prices for such a trip have increased, but not unreasonably. For a guide, boat, all equipment, plus the gourmet trout lunch (cooked with bacon over an open fire), expect to pay about $225 for two people. One final note about trout fishing on the McKenzie. You can only keep hatchery fish. The native fish must be released.

RAFTING. There are good white-water runs through Class II and III rapids that last from half a day to two full days. Rafting trips are seven to 25 miles long and often include the notorious Martins Rapids below Vida. Prices vary but count on about $60 per person for a half-day and $110 for a full day of rafting. Lunches are usually included.

HOT BATHS. Almost worth a trip in itself is **Belknap Lodge and Hot Springs**. On a reach of zestful white McKenzie water, this lodge and attendant hot springs is entirely restored. The cabins are inexpensive and the comfortable rooms are moderately priced. Belknap is located at milepost 56.

HIKING. The **McKenzie River Trail** runs for about 25 miles and starts just beyond the town of McKenzie Bridge. You should pick up maps from the ranger station in Blue River and choose the appropriate section of this trail. The five-mile hike around this lake (you can drive too) is beautiful.

For a short, easy hike, drive up the old McKenzie Pass Road, just five miles beyond McKenzie Bridge, and continue 10 miles to the sign announcing **Proxy Falls**. The walk to both Upper Proxy and Lower Proxy Falls is less than a mile. It is a pleasant stroll through forests of fir, hemlock, vine maple, and rhododendron. This area is closed in winter.

For a more energetic trek, continue up the old McKenzie Pass Road past Proxy Falls for another 10 or so miles, and then turn west on Road 1532. You should keep going until you reach Scott Lake Camp. The camp is about 72 miles east of Eugene. You can park and walk the **Scott Mountain Trail**. It goes through pleasant meadows, past Benson Lake, and then climbs the mountain slope. The one-way distance is three miles, the gain in elevation is 1,246 feet and the summit is 6,116 feet. In the early summer, there are mosquitoes in this area.

DINING. There are two restaurants in Vida. The tiny, informal **Village Café** has excellent hamburgers, sandwiches, chili and wonderful pie at very modest prices. The **Riverside Inn,** which has overnight accommodations, offers leisurely fireside dining at moderate prices.

Further up the river at milepost 50 and the McKenzie Bridge, the **Log Cabin** offers both lunch and dinner. The moderately priced food, including venison and buffalo steaks, is excellent. Overnight cabins are available.

TRANSPORTATION. From Eugene, the Lane County Transit System has busses that serve the McKenzie as far as McKenzie Bridge (50 miles). They make a lot of stops, but there's plenty of local color. The fare is about $5.

Up the Willamette Valley from Eugene to Portland

Driving north up I-5, from Eugene to Portland, takes about two hours. Other than the distant mountains to the east and west, this 120-mile trip bypasses most towns and runs through flat country. It's a land where sheep graze, where grass seed and corn are grown, and where orchards flourish.

To see the best of the Willamette Valley, visitors need to use less-traveled roads such as Highways 99W and 99E. Out of Eugene, I recommend taking 99, the road that runs through Junction City to the peaceful riverside town of Harrisburg (which has an unusually good restaurant called the Vault). From there the road winds through bottomlands of green fields, flanked by stands of oak and maple, rather than Douglas fir. The country here looks more like the Midwest than Oregon.

You should consult a map, and stay on these secondary roads. Follow an easy route north and pass through Corvallis, Monmouth, Rickreal, Amity, McMinnville, and Newberg. In time, you'll end up in Portland.

You might consider a more in-depth, adventurous approach to this area – the river. This is the slow, infrequently taken (at least all the way) means of seeing the Willamette Valley. It can be hard, and it is sometimes hot work. This is the way much of the area was first seen and, thanks to the Willamette River Greenway Authority, the river is now as it once was.

RAFTING AND CANOEING. I have a 14-foot inflatable raft (with rowing frame) that I've used over selected passages of both the McKenzie and Willamette Rivers. I've done most of the Willamette, all the way to Portland, and can report that the river is easy to navigate. There are only a few riffles near the Eugene end, and the lower river can be slow going. Sustained rowing is sometimes required. The river has an overpowering, serene beauty and an unusual population of wildlife. If you liked Mark Twain's *Huckleberry Finn*, you'll love the Willamette River.

Assume then that we've put our raft in the water (fully provisioned with food, assorted beverages, sleeping bags and life jackets) at Armitage Park, on the McKenzie near Eugene. We start at a fair clip and go down the last of the McKenzie River. Judging from the rocks on the bottom of this clear running stream, we are moving about as fast as a person can jog. Thirty minutes later a confusion of cottonwood-clad islands appear. Passing through them, we are now on the Willamette River. We are now on the Willamette River Greenway and 165 water miles from Portland.

From here to Harrisburg is a meandering 21 miles. Little paddling is required so the area's beauty can be enjoyed without hard work. Still, the river does tricky things. Fast water on the outside of turns can push you toward the shore, where fallen logs jut out into the river. Getting hung up on one of these logs could pull a boat under the log. Even if the current doesn't require that you row, you must paddle to avoid these logs. Along this stretch of the river there are parks, landings and many tiny islands where you can camp.

If you start your trip in the morning, you will reach **Harrisburg** (just past a pair of bridges) in time for lunch. It is about a five-hour trip. I suggest that you pull your raft up at the Harrisburg Park River Landing and then wander up the street for lunch at **The Vault**.

Harrisburg to Peoria is 14 miles and too far to go this first day. You should continue on another four or five winding miles beyond Harrisburg and check out some of the tiny islands in this area. Choose one of the islands, set up camp, build a fire, maybe go for a swim, and settle in for the night.

The next day is a good 20-mile drift to Corvallis. But on the way, pause for a stroll through the sleepy hamlet of Peoria. Nearing Corvallis, the river becomes wider and a little slower. Corvallis is a good place to stop for the night. Pull into Michael's Landing at the north end of town and arrange for a safe place to put the boat before you check into a motel.

Corvallis

Population 44,800

This attractive town, with its traditional main street and the classic Benton County Courthouse, has been classified as one of the prime places to live in the U.S. Here you will find the wooded, green, dignified campus of Oregon State University. The alumni refer to themselves as "Beavers born, beavers bred and when we die we'll be beavers dead."

ACCOMMODATIONS. The **Best Western** (☎ 503-758-8571) has moderate rates. The **Ramada Inn** (☎ 503-753-9151) has a restaurant, cocktail lounge and evening dancing. Their rates are moderate. Rates at the **Shanico Inn** (☎ 503-754-7474) are inexpensive.

FOOD. A stroll through town will reveal good places. At the river, consider **Michael's Landing** for steaks, seafood and cocktails. For Mexican food, go to **Papagayos**.

Albany

Population 29,500

Beyond Corvallis the river becomes somewhat wider and slower. But you shouldn't be in a great hurry to cover the required 11 miles. The scenery here is lush and green. Watch for ospreys and herons. With the current and only a little rowing, the trip takes about seven hours. There are four landings or parks (with some camping amenities) on this run.

Albany, particularly the part seen from the river, has connections with the past. From the 1880's up until 1910, steamboats arrived here with passengers from Portland (120 miles away). They then took trains to other destinations.

More than 500 of Albany's historic buildings remain. The buildings can be toured with the assistance of brochures obtained from the Albany Visitors' Center. **Bryant Park**, where you'll land, is one of the historic attractions.

ACCOMMODATIONS. If you drive to Albany, the best motels are away from the center of town and a considerable distance from the river. Most motels, such as the following two, are off I-5. The

Comfort Inn (☎ 503-928-0921), at exit 234A, has moderate rates. At exit 223, the **Motel** Orleans (☎ 503-926-0170) has inexpensive rates.

If you arrive by boat, you may have to take a taxi or otherwise negotiate a ride to a motel. You should consider camping by the river at **Hyak Park,** which is just a few miles away from Albany.

FOOD. Try **Pop's Branding Iron** or, for a touch of Italy, the **First Round Tavern**. The **Burgundy** is for more sophisticated dining.

Salem
Population 107,800

From Albany to Salem is about 38 water miles and too far for a day's drift. This is the farm heartland of Oregon. It is where the Willamette curves lazily along tree-fringed shores that should be savored and used for camping.

You might explore the pair of islands which are six and eight miles north of Albany. At Luckiamute Landing (at the mouth of the Luckiamute River) there's a place to camp.

Set out the next day and float past the Buena Vista Ferry crossing. This free ferry, which has been in existence since 1851, is about four miles west of I-5 at exit 242. It connects with Independence and Monmouth. Just beyond the ferry there is an island called **Well's Island Park**, which offers good camping. At this point you're three miles beyond Luckiamute and only 95 miles from Portland.

Independence is 11 miles north of Wells Island Park and there are few campsites. You may want to hitch a ride to Monmouth (population 6,300 and only a few miles away), where you will find Western Oregon State College and the **Courtesy Inn**, which is a good, inexpensive place to stay and dine.

From Independence, Salem is 12 water miles away. It's a good day's run past an island or two and several non-camping landings. In Salem you'll be ready for a shower, a good bed, and a restaurant. Pull into **Wallace Marine Park**, just across the river from downtown Salem. Be sure to ask someone to watch your raft.

Salem, which was settled in 1834, is the state's capital and the third largest city in Oregon. It is an attractive city, a place of well-designed plazas, majestic Capitol grounds and public parks with miles of bike and foot paths. This is also home to the dignified, tree-shaded campus of Willamette University, noted for law, liberal arts and music. If you are coming in by car from I-5, you will see Oregon's austere penitentiary.

At a Distance from Salem

The Enchanted Forest is about eight miles outside of Salem, just off I-5 at exit 248. Here there are rides of all kinds, haunted houses, and fairy-tale cottages. It isn't Disneyland, but everyone seems to enjoy it.

Silver Falls State Park. To reach this park from Salem, you should take Highway 22 east for seven miles, then turn north on Road 214. You then follow the signs to the park (about 14 miles). Silver Falls is one of Oregon's most beautiful spots, and it's a great place to walk. You might walk the **Trail of 10 Falls**, a seven-mile loop that takes you past stands of old growth timber, waterfalls and through a natural garden of ferns and mossy rocks. The park also offers 52 full-amenity camping sites.

The North Santiam Canyon. This canyon is reached by taking Highway 22 east. You might want to pause at Stayton, about 16 miles later, and examine the historic Jordan covered bridge in **Pioneer Park**.

Then you continue on another 30 or so miles, past Detroit Lake, and turn left on Road 46. Follow the signs to **Breitenbush Hot Spring**. In addition to the hot spring, there are good trails, inexpensive cabins, and simple food.

To go from Salem to Portland by river, you will cover 75 beautiful and varied miles. The river is now wider and the current gentle. This means that rowing must be done, particularly if a breeze is blowing from the north. There are some interesting islands to explore north of Salem and there is a good place to camp at **Spring Valley Access** (about 10 miles from Salem). The Wheatland Ferry comes three or four miles later.

It is another 15 miles from the Wheatland Ferry to St. Paul. Be sure to avoid the tricky Lambert Slough, which leads off to the left just past the ferry. The scenery is great along here as the river winds past a number of beautiful islands before it reaches Yamhill Landing, where there are camping amenities. At this point, you are near the historic towns of St. Paul and Dayton. Here there are churches and other buildings from the mid-1800s. Newberg, not right on the river, is another eight miles and you are now 40 water miles from Portland.

ACCOMMODATIONS. Coming into Salem (along I-5) you'll see very good motels on either side of the freeway; but, for the best of Salem, go into town. A block or two from downtown, right across from the Civic Center, try the **City Center Motel** (☎ 503-581-4441). There are lots of restaurants near the motel and its rates are inexpensive. The **Tiki Lodge**, at 3705 Market, is another inexpensive and good place to stay. And at similar rates, try the **Best Western** on Pacific Highway (☎ 503-390-3200) or the **Salem Super 8 Motel** (☎ 503-370-8888).

FOOD. There are almost limitless possibilities for dining. Locals are enthusiastic about the moderately priced continental cuisine offered at the **Inn at Orchard Heights**. It is at 695 Orchard Heights Road. The moderately priced **Chumaree Comfortel** has entertainment as well as food. **Mazzis** on Commercial Street has good Italian food at modest prices. **Cheers**, on 2410 Mission S.E., describes itself as the "newest place to play." It provides games as well as steaks, spirits, salads, and good hamburgers. The dinners are moderately priced. **Burt Lee's Tahiti** offers moderately priced seafood, steaks and poultry cooked with Polynesian seasonings. For evening entertainment and a lively bar, go to the **Night Deposit**. It is at 195 Commercial Street and serves dinners of steak, seafood or poultry. Moderate.

Newberg

Population 13,100

If you arrive in Newberg by car, on 99W, the road enters town a stone's throw from where Herbert Hoover lived with his aunt and uncle in 1884. The house he lived in, the **Hoover-Minthorn House**, is now a museum that contains photos and material from that era. The house is on S. River and E. 2nd Streets. Admission is $1-$1.50.

Nearby is the school Hoover attended. In those days it was a Quaker institution called Pacific Academy. Now it is named for the founder of the Quakers and is known as George Fox College.

Today, Newberg is a quiet town. It is an attractive community, filled with old homes that reflect its sober, conservative past. The campus of George Fox is near the center of town, along with the imposing belfry spire of the Old Friends Church.

But times change and, despite its sober background, Newberg is now surrounded by more than 18 wineries.

You can spend a couple of days seeing these wineries and the pastoral lands they occupy. Write for a free map from The Oregon Winegrowers Association, 1200 N.W. Front Avenue, Suite 400, Portland, OR 97209.

Most of the wineries are small, family-owned vineyards that produce award-winning vintages of Riesling, Chardonnay, Pinot Grigio, Pinot Noir, Sauvignon Blanc, Gewurtztraminer, and others. Start in Newberg with the **Rex Hill Vineyards**, then drive west on 99W for a few miles until you reach Dundee, which is also known for its orchards of plums, prunes and walnuts. In Dundee, visit the **Sokol Blosser Winery**. Then drive into the Red Hills and taste Pinot Noir at the **Eyrie Vineyards**.

Continue on to McMinnville, home of Linfield College, and have lunch or dinner, accompanied by some of the regional wines, at **Nick's Italian Café**. It is a favorite restaurant among the locals. Near McMinniville, S.W. of town, you may taste Pinot Noir, Riesling, and others, at the **Yamhill Valley Vineyards**. Then, traveling south on 99W, you enter the peaceful little town of Amity. Try the wines at **Amity Vineyards**. There is much more to see. This is where a detailed map comes in handy. With it, you will have access to some of the most delightful byways in the Pacific Northwest.

FOOD AND ACCOMMODATIONS. For meals and accommodations, the **Partridge Farm Bed and Breakfast** (☎ 503-528-2050), at 4300 E. Portland Road, is excellent. You might also try the **Smith House Bed and Breakfast** (☎ 503-538-1115), at 415 N. College Street. The **Shilo Inn** (☎ 503-537-0303), at 501 Sitka Avenue, is near several restaurants. The prices at all three are moderate.

BACK TO THE RIVER. From the Newberg Boat Ramp, the river runs straight (but it is still scenic) for six miles, until it reaches **Champoeg Park**. In this manicured park, you will find good camping facilities, with many amenities.

Champoeg was the place where the provisional government for the first American Commonwealth in the Pacific Northwest was formed in 1843. It was also from Champoeg that areas to the south were explored by river.

Going downriver to the north, the waters become busy (but it is still beautiful and filled with river life) as it runs past a number of river accesses, marinas and parks. Few of these landings permit overnight camping as much of the shore is private property. So, for camping, you are (not unhappily) relegated to islands.

At Oregon City, about 15 miles from Portland, there is a slight glitch. There are falls here, substantial ones, and you will have to pass through locks. These locks, in operation since 1873, are open for use – free of charge – from 8am to 12pm, seven days a week. Chances are you can pass through along with a commercial vessel, but don't count on it. Put ashore above the locks at **Rock Island Landing**, which has camping facilities, and call the Lock Master at tel. 655-3381. He'll assign a time for the one-hour passage through the locks.

Oregon City

Population 14,700

Oregon City, where the river plunges an inhospitable 40 feet, was the first capital of the Territory and it was considered the end of The Oregon Trail. Step ashore in this old town and take the free elevator that lifts pedestrians to an observation deck overlooking the falls and the city.

Beyond Oregon City the river is busier. Portland is getting closer and overnight camping is more difficult. Still, beauty prevails and there are lots of well used parks and marinas that offer daytime sustenance.

By now you have done the Willamette River – congratulations – and a take-out place is in order. I suggest the Staff Jennings Marina on the west end of the Sellwood Bridge.

Central Oregon

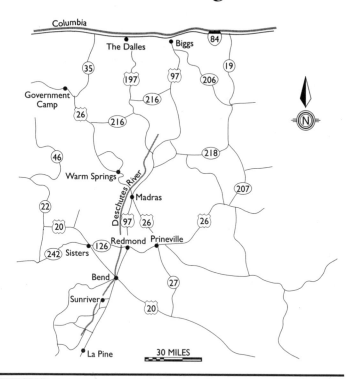

Central Oregon

The Dalles is the northern gateway to Central Oregon. Read this chapter backwards if you're coming from California.

From Portland to The Dalles along I-30 (The Columbia Gorge again) is an easily done 112 miles. It's a curious trip, a run that passes through heavy green coniferous forests and abruptly ends with open patches of land spotted with sagebrush. At The Dalles the forest is gone. This is the edge of the Oregon desert where the grasslands, the wheat fields, the grazing lands of central and eastern Oregon begin.

The Dalles

Population 11,100

Lying in a bend of the Columbia River, where there once were turbulent rapids, this town began as a fur trading center, continued as a stop on the Oregon Trail, became a Gold Rush boom town in the 1860's and finally emerged as the agricultural center it is today.

Because of the rapids, early French voyageurs called this town Les Dalles, meaning "flagstones." Now, because of The Dalles Dam three miles upstream, the rapids are submerged and passenger boats, pleasure craft and barges loaded with wheat ply the river with ease.

Step into the **Visitor's Information Center** at 901 E. 2nd Street and pick up maps that will lead you to scenes of earlier days – to the old Courthouse, circa 1858, to a pair of 19th-century churches, to the remnants of Fort Dalles, built in 1850.

For windsurfing, boating and fishing, visit nearby **Riverfront Park**. For Indian lore, drive east of town – near the dam – where Indians once speared Chinook salmon at now submerged Celilo Falls. Then look at an Oregon road map and notice how Highways 187 and 97 run south along the eastern slope of the Cascade Range – close to much extravagant beauty – and end up at the California border near Klamath Falls.

ACCOMMODATIONS AND FOOD. Right in town, within walking distance of the central restaurants, the **Tapadero Inn** (☎ 503-296-9107), with moderate rates, is entirely comfortable. It has a pool and a very agreeable restaurant. **The Quality Inn** (☎ 503-298-5161), with a farm theme restaurant, is 1½ miles west off I-84. Moderate. **The Shilo Inn** (☎ 503-298-5502) has views and a good restaurant. Moderate.

Moving south from The Dalles, Highway 187 winds through hills of sagebrush dotted with ponderosa pine and junipers – cowboy country – to Dufur, Tygh Valley, Maupin and finally Madras, about 100 miles south of The Dalles.

Madras

Population 3,400

I can think of four good reasons to stop at or near this high desert town on Highway 97, a continuance of Highway 187. They are rockhounding, river running, boating, fishing and access to the Warm Springs Indian Reservation.

ROCKHOUNDING. Visit the **Madras-Jefferson County Chamber of Commerce** at 197 S.E. 5th St. Ask for maps and guidance to areas where agates, petrified wood fossils and gemstones are found. Better yet, ask where you can find thunder eggs. These are the curious lava-born rocks that, when cut open and polished, reveal a multihued dramatic interior.

RIVER RUNNING. The Deschutes River is a varied, complex stream that arises in the southern Cascades and winds its way through canyons where rattlesnakes lurk, through desert, pine forests and lava flows all the way to the Columbia River. Here in the Madras area – to the east about 15 miles – the Deschutes travels about 100 miles (often turbulently) through deep canyons to the Columbia River near The Dalles.

From the above junctions, on Highway 26 about 12 miles west of Madras, rafters do runs of up to five days, as far as Sherar Bridge, 50 miles to the north near Maupin. This is not a trip for novices. Unless you're whitewater wise it's best to join a group with guide. Bring fishing gear too. This is a productive trout area.

Beyond Sherar Bridge, downriver another 45 miles is another stretch of dramatic canyons and rugged desert land.

Contact **Oregon River Experiences Inc**. 2 Jefferson Parkway, #D7, Lake Oswego, OR 97035. Expect to pay about $330 for a five-day trip.

BOATING AND FISHING. Where the Metolius and the Deschutes meet west of Madras, there is a dam and a lake has formed. This is **Lake Billy Chinook**. Fishing from the shore is good or boats can be rented.

THE WARM SPRINGS INDIAN RESERVATION, 16 miles N.W. of Madras on Highway 26 is the 640,000-acre reservation of The

Confederate Tribes of the Warm Springs Indians. Using money from the U.S. Government in settlement for the loss of their traditional fishing on the Columbia River when the dam was put in, these Indians have built a complex that should be seen – and enjoyed. In what looks like a movie version of Indian country, you can visit the Tribal Information Center to soak up Indian lore and buy woven baskets, beadwork and leather goods. From time to time, traditional Indian baked salmon is served. Horses are available for rides into the hills, and hot mineral baths are at hand for soothing sore muscles. Trout fishing in both the Deschutes and Warm Springs Rivers is good. For RV camping there's an area providing full hook-ups.

ACCOMMODATIONS. There are two extremely good resorts in the area. Both are about 10 miles north of the town of Warm Springs, at the village of Kahneeta. **Kah-Neet-Ta Lodge** (☎ 503-553-1112) has everything you might want – fine food, fishing, bicycling, horseback riding and jogging trails. Expensive. **Kah-Neet-Ta Village** (☎ 503-553-1112), in a natural setting on the Warm Springs River, has all amenities at expensive rates.

Some of the best camping in Central Oregon is at **The Cove Pinnacles Campground**. It has facilities for 87 full RV hook-ups, 91 electrical hook-ups, and 94 tents. Here too there is a general store, a marina, and outstanding views.

FROM MADRAS. Continuing south from Madras about two miles along Highway 97, there is an important detour – Highway 26, running 27 miles S.E., through juniper-dotted rangeland to Prineville and to the nearby Ochoco National Forest (see below).

Prineville

Population 5,400

This self-contained town at 2,868 feet elevation supports itself comfortably on agriculture, cattle, wood products and on what rockhounds, fisherman, hunters, cross-country skiers, hikers and the curious bring in. Used as a gateway to neighboring attractions, Prineville is an ideal stop.

ACCOMMODATION AND DINING. The Rustlers Roost Motel (☎ 503-447-4185), 960 W. 3rd Street, offers cowboy style and Western comfort. It has good food. Rates are inexpensive. **The Ochoco**

Inn and Motel (☎ 503-447-6231), 123 E. 3rd Street, has a restaurant-cocktail bar plus full comforts at inexpensive rates.

Nearby Attractions

THE OCHOCO NATIONAL FOREST. To get at a representative portion of this remote area drive east on Highway 26 about 12 miles to Ochoco Reservoir – which has RV camping and good fishing. Turn left to the north on Mill Creek Road for about 12 miles to the **Mill Creek Wilderness Area**. Note along this road the 300-foot stone spire known as Stein's Pillar. Then pull up in the rugged ponderosa-lodgepole terrain of Mill Creek. Here there are clear-running mountain streams full of trout and bass, plus a local population of deer, elk, coyotes, magpies, quails and raccoons.

In this area, and the next 25-30 miles on either side of Highway 26, there are more than 60 miles of trails that are perfect for informal camping. Go prepared for the wilderness; you're well removed from humanity here.

PRINEVILLE RESERVOIR. Drive south from Prineville about 20 miles to this lake, formed by a dam on the Crooked River. This is a favored destination of discriminating Oregonians who love fishing in an area of austere beauty. I know people in Eugene who drive their RV's on a pilgrimage each summer to this lake. They blissfully settle in at water's edge under the junipers and here they camp, swim, fish and fraternize with other happy campers. When they return home their freezer is filled with the bounty of this lake.

UP THE CROOKED RIVER. Do an all-day backroad trip along the Crooked River to Paulina, continue on four miles to the east and turn north to remote **Wolf Creek Campground**, where there's RV camping, fishing, and hiking. From here you can make a loop back to Highway 26 and return to Prineville. You'll have done well over 100 attention-getting miles.

Returning to the important north-south Highway 97, take Highway 126 from Prineville to Redmond.

Redmond

Population 3,007

Climbing Monkey Face at Smith Rock State Park.

This is another high desert juniper-sagebrush town where cattle, lumber, ranching and dairy farming is practiced. It's a fine place to stop but you're close to Bend or Sisters and may just want to spend a day doing the local attractions. One of these is a must.

Smith Rock State Park. Go north on 97 to Terrebonne, about five miles. Turn east another three miles to the park. This is an eerily beautiful, starkly cliffed area through which the Crooked River runs. It is a challenging place for rock climbers, a wonderful spot for picnicking, with a leisurely seven miles of walking at the base of these rocks along the river. It's open from dawn to dusk.

After this, you're poised to continue west along 126 to Sisters, Black Butte, the Mt. Jefferson Wilderness Area – or south only 16 miles to the near-metropolis of Bend. However, with the Central Oregon-Cascade Wilderness in mind, this may be the time to consider the Pacific Crest Trail.

The Pacific Crest Trail

Running from Washington's border with Canada, the Pacific Crest Trail passes down the Cascades of Oregon and Washington, then all the way through California to the Mexican border. The trail's total length is 2,400 miles. Oregon has nearly 450 of those miles.

I don't know anyone personally who's done it all of the trail in one go, but some stalwart souls have done it and written about the experience. One excellent account involving all three states has been written by William R. Gray, photographed by Sam Abell and published by the National Geographic Society. It's good reading.

I only know people (myself included) who have done selected portions of the trail. We don't have the discipline and stamina to manage 10-15 miles a day over perhaps 40 days. We are the kind who drive in where major roads cross the trail and set out for modest distances to a host of wonderful destinations.

As mentioned earlier, under The Columbia Gorge, the Pacific Crest Trail goes south from near Cascade Locks on the Columbia River and climbs up several thousand feet, winding through dense forests, along rushing streams, through canyons and close to pristine Lost Lake. The trail then crosses the flank of Mt. Hood and continues on into the Mt. Jefferson Wilderness Area. At this point, dedicated hikers will have covered nearly a hundred miles.

You can drive into the Mt. Jefferson and Mt. Washington Wilderness Areas. We drive in from Redmond or Bend, along Highway 20 – about 20 miles.

Sisters

Population 700

Set in pine woods on the eastern slope of the Santiam Pass, this town has a tourist-oriented frontier flavor. There are wooden sidewalks, western-style saloons, western art galleries, chuckwagon restaurants and, at the edge of town, Patterson's Ranch has one of the largest llama herds in North America.

Sisters is a well-situated springboard to the best of Central Oregon's Wilderness areas.

ACCOMMODATION AND DINING. Choices. Stay right in Sisters at the **Best Western Ponderosa Lodge** (☎ 503-549-1234), with moderate rates. Have fine chuckwagon meals in town at **The Gallery Restaurant**. Dinners are inexpensive. For the best known place in town, try **The Hotel** Sisters Restaurant. This is a 1912 hotel that's been brought back to life as an intimate place to dine. They serve steaks, ribs, Mexican food, chicken, and cocktails. Dinners are moderately priced.

Some 20 miles west of Sisters, at **Camp Sherman**, where the idyllic Metolios River is born, there are the **Metolius River Lodges** (☎ 503-595-6290). They have cabins with cooking facilities at moderate rates. For dining or staying at Camp Sherman there's the **Cold Spring Resort** (☎ 503-595-6271). Rates are moderate. There's also a full RV hookup at Cold Spring.

At **Black Butte**, about 10 miles west of Sisters, there is the prestigious **Butte Properties** (☎ 503-549-3433), complete with fine restaurant and all possible amenities – skiing, golf, tennis, and horseback riding. Rates are moderate to luxury.

From any of these places you're well positioned to explore the wilderness areas.

The Mt. Jefferson Wilderness Area

Fishing at Marion Lake, Mt. Jefferson Wilderness Area.

The Pacific Crest Trail crosses Highway 20 just west of the 4,817-foot Santiam Pass. Here, as you proceed north (only in high summer), the trail leads through a 36-mile stretch of lava flows, under the rock needles of 7,841-foot Three Fingered Jack, past waterfalls, one gem-like lake after another and, finally, along the western slope of Mt. Jefferson.

Go into these areas well prepared. Have Topographic maps, leave word at the trailhead when you leave about when you plan to return. Observe local rules about fires and camping spots and carry out all your trash.

The Mt. Washington Wilderness Area

To get at this area, go west from Sisters for 21 miles on Highway 20. Turn left (south) on Road 2960 for about three miles. From here, the Pacific Crest Trail goes south for 13 miles to the McKenzie Pass Road (Highway 242), which is closed in winter.

Hiking this trail provides nearly everything – meadows, lava flows, coniferous forest, Big Lake, Little Belknap Crater, great views – and, for hardy, experienced rock climbers, the scramble up the rock chimneys and pinnacles of 7,802-foot Mt. Washington is a worthy challenge. There are plenty of campsites on this walk – but it's best to carry your own water.

Unless you want to retrace the 13 miles, arrange a car shuttle. Plan to end the hike at the Dee Wright Observatory on Highway 242. The observatory, set in an eight-mile-long lava flow, is 15 miles west of Sisters.

The Three Sisters Wilderness Area

Within this 208,500-acre preserve, ranging from about 2,000 to 10,385 feet elevation, there are trails leading in all directions – nearly 300 miles of trails, to say nothing of the Pacific Crest Trail that runs through here for about 40 miles.

This preserve, about 34 miles from north to south, offers a highly popular spectrum of activities – simple day hikes, substantial back packing, winter cross-country skiing, mountain climbing, fishing and superb photography. The character of this terrain is varied too. Walkers, even those who only drive to trailheads, will move about in forests of Douglas fir (on the western side), ponderosa pine (on the eastern side) and nearly everywhere among groves of spruce, cedar, hemlock and a startling variety of wildflowers. Looming over all of this are the snow-capped Three Sisters mountains and their attendant 16 glaciers. South Sister rises up 10,358 feet, North Sister 10,094 feet, and Middle Sister is 10,053 feet. In addition, there's 9,175-foot Broken Top.

All three of the Sisters attract climbers. South Sister is a gentler climb, while North Sister is the roughest. There are those who take pride in ascending all three peaks in the same day. I have so far successfully resisted that temptation.

To get at the Three Sisters Wilderness Area, there are four options:

1. From the north on the McKenzie Pass Road (Highway 242) there are several trails, including the Pacific Crest Trail, that take you from, or near, the Dee Wright Observatory, 15 miles west of the Sisters. Using Topographical maps of the Three Sisters Wilderness Area, you can take the short 1.2-mile stroll through wild rhododendrons and huckleberries to a pair of memorable cascades – **Upper** and **Lower Proxy Falls**. The trails branch off Highway 242, eight miles east of its junctions with Highway 126.

2. A more substantial undertaking is **Camp Lake Trek**. This starts just east of Sisters on Highway 242. It's a seven-mile walk to this popular lake. There are plenty of places to camp there or en route. More importantly, Camp Lake is one of the best setting-out places for climbing all Three Sisters.

3. From the west on Highway 126 (the road from Eugene), just east of Blue River, a road turns south to Cougar Reservoir. Trails lead into the area from there. For example, you can go to 5,708-foot **Olallie Mountain**, about four miles, or beyond to Yankee Mountain. Views from these elevations are beyond words.

4. Running southwest from Bend, the Cascade Lakes Highway (also called Century Drive) does a 100-mile scenic loop. In this case the term "scenic loop" is an understatement. Put this road on your "must do" list.

Mt. Bachelor, 9,065 feet, only 22 miles southwest of Bend, is a premiere ski resort. With snow that lasts through mid-summer it's easy to see why skiers of ability are drawn here. Mt. Bachelor has 60 downhill runs, 10 lifts and an extensive cross country trail system.

ACCOMMODATIONS AND DINING. Six miles out of Bend, 18 miles from Mt. Bachelor, check out **Mt. Bachelor Village** (☎ 503-389-5900). It has a restaurant, cocktail lounge and sports amenities at moderate to expensive rates.

Continuing down the Cascade Lakes Highway there are unlimited Forest Service campgrounds, many that have trailheads leading to the interior or with serene walks around the lakes, such as Sparks, Elk, Cultus, Crane Prairie, Wickiup and Davis. Some of these lakes have rustic lodges, friendly places with hearty food. Check out the **Cultus Lake Resort,** ☎ 503-389-3230, with moderate rates.

For serious treks into the Sisters back country, pack animals are available at these stops.

Along Highway 58, the road that from Eugene to Chemult in Central Oregon (100 miles), drive west just past Willamette Pass (easily found on road maps), then turn north on the road to Waldo Lake and examine trail possibilities. There are many, some on the Pacific Crest Trail.

Snowboarding on Mt. Bachelor.

Note: Go into all of these wilderness areas equipped with Topographical maps. Write **The Forest Supervisor, Deschutes National Forest,** 211 N.E. Revere St., Bend OR 97701.

Bend

Population 20,500

Back on Highway 97 heading south toward California, Bend is a rewarding stop. It's a town with an unusual blend of sophistication, creature comforts and western-style horsiness. It boasts 300 days of sunshine a year and offers proximity to the activities sportsmen require.

As with most of Central Oregon, Bend is far different from what you find on the western slopes of the Cascades. In the west, the landscape is lush, varied and often wet. Bend is in pinewood, sagebrush, and juniper country. It's more open, free from underbrush, arid land, often dotted with lava flows and volcanic cinders. Winters are cold, summers are warm and aromatic.

You will find good restaurants and fine accommodations here. There is pleasant strolling around a city center park and lake or along a bend in the Deschutes River (where the city gets its name), but you may be more interested in some of the attractions outside of town.

ACCOMMODATIONS. Bend abounds with motels, more than 30 of them, many in plain sight as you drive into town on 97. Rates vary from inexpensive to moderate.

One of two places I've always enjoyed because of their beautiful setting and proximity to town is **The Riverhouse, ☎** 503-389-3111, 3075 N. Highway 97. The Riverhouse has three restaurants and a lounge with live entertainment, jogging paths and golf course. Rates are moderate. The other is **The Bend Riverside Motel, ☎** 503-389-2363, 1565 N.W. Hill Street. It is next to attractive Pioneer Park, within walking distance of town. Rates are moderate.

FOOD. The Pine Tavern, 967 N.W. Brooks Street, has been around for more than 70 years. With a view of the park, this place serves fine continental-American food at moderate prices. **Pescatore**, 119 N.W. Minnesota Avenue, serves northern Italian food at modest prices. **Players Grille** prices are modest. **Mexicali Rose**, 301 N.E. Franklin, is certified as one of Oregon's best Mexican restaurants. Prices are modest. **Giuseppe's Ristorante**, 932 N.W. Bond St., is a popular, modestly priced Italian place.

There are plenty of other places to eat. Stroll through town and check out the deli's and the fast food places. Don't neglect the three restaurants at the **Riverhouse Motel**.

SOUTH FROM BEND. Driving south from Bend through patchy, low pine woods, watch for the **High Desert Museum**. It's about six miles south of Bend. Here, within 150 acres of carefully guarded natural habitat, this museum exhibits local Indian artifacts, identifies flora and fauna and displays regional wildlife. Along the self-guiding footpaths, life in the high desert is thoroughly explored. Admission is $3.50; children, $2.75.

A few miles beyond the High Desert Museum, the **Lava River Cave State Park** appears. At this cave, which is a mile-long lava tube, you can rent lanterns and walk through what used to be a volcano.

Sunriver

Population 1,100

This community, set in a pine woods, lies along a peaceful stretch of the Deschutes River. It's just 15 miles south of Bend.

The people who live here, many retired, and the people who come to stay in rental condominiums are entirely dedicated to the pursuit of fun. They ride about on bicycles or horses, play tennis and golf, canoe on the Deschutes and in winter they're close to skiing at nearby Mt. Bachelor. Nobody wears a frown at Sunriver. I think it's illegal.

ACCOMMODATIONS AND FOOD. The Sunriver Lodge and Resort, ☎ 503-593-1221, has everything and anything required at moderate to expensive rates. The Lodge, which is in a forest setting, can provide either rooms or condo-townhouse facilities. It has golf, tennis, bicycles, a boat dock, a health club, two heated pools, dining room, cocktail lounge, entertainment, conference facilities – and it's hard by an airstrip.

Apart from the Lodge there are rental condos available. For information, call **Central Oregon Reservations,** ☎ 1-800-000-8334.

SIGHTS. Newberry Crater is 24 miles south of Bend, plus another 13 miles to the east on Road 21. This immense crater, a volcanic monument, is also the scene of two lakes – Paulina and East Lake. Fishing is said to be good there, as are the rustic resorts and public campgrounds. In winter this is an outstanding place for snowmobiling.

Further south on Highway 97, just past the town of La Pine – about 10 miles beyond the turnoff to Newberry Crater – watch for Highway 31 which goes S.E. If it's close to lunch time go prepared for a picnic in one of the loneliest, most desert-bound places in Oregon. This is the ancient volcanic rim called **Fort Rock**, now a state park. It's about 35 miles from the Highway 97 turnoff, plus another eight or nine miles to the left. You'll see it clearly marked on road maps.

Crossing this open, sagebrush-littered land, you'll see Fort Rock miles before you get there. The 360-foot walls of the rock and its half-mile width dominate the surrounding desert. On arrival, park your car and walk into the rim through the side that has been eroded away. Sit for awhile inside the walls of the "fort," try to comprehend the passage of time and listen to the sound of silence.

In the 30's it was in this area – rich in archaeological artifacts – that the late Luther Cressman, a University of Oregon anthropologist (and Margaret Mead's first husband), found several man-made sandals that were determined by carbon dating to be over 9,000 years old.

About eight miles N.W. of Fort Rock, on a road that leads back toward Highway 97, there is another dramatic remnant of the past. It's called **Hole-in-the-Ground**. This is a symmetrical, steep-sided hole 300 feet deep. Some think that a meteor hit the earth here. Others, backed by more hardcore science, say it's a volcanic "blow-out." Nevertheless, it's an eerie place. Standing at the rim, you can often see game – deer and elk feeding in the bottom of the hole. There are also some colorful caves in the area, supporting the volcanic theory of the hole's origin.

Back on Highway 97, 26 miles south of La Pine, Highway 58 (coming from Eugene) appears. Turning right on Highway 58, about 25 miles will bring you to a pair of fine lakes – **Crescent** and **Odell** – and another part of the Pacific Crest Trail.

These two glacial lakes, beautiful, ancient and cold, are blessed with good fishing and, because of the winds, offer good sailing.

The Odell Lake Resort, ☎ 503-432-2540, is near the Odell exit off Highway 58. With restaurant, fishing equipment and sailboats for rent, plus access to hiking trails, this is a vacation destination in itself.

Crater Lake

And so we come to one of the prime destinations in North America – Crater Lake. This is a place that causes gasps when first seen.

To get there – shown plainly on all road maps – turn right (west) from Highway 97 onto Road 138, for 15 miles. Then drive south another nine miles to the lake. Use this road in summer only. In winter, an all-weather road (#62), well to the south, goes to the lake.

Crater Lake is what remains of Mt. Mazama, a 12,000-foot volcano that erupted about 8,000 years ago and caused the mountain to collapse. This created the caldera that is now the lake. What we see today is an unbelievably blue lake, about four miles by six (with a 26-mile shoreline) lying at the base of 500- to 2,000-foot lava cliffs. The depth of the lake is 1,932 feet.

Surrounding this most unusual lake, more awesome than beautiful, the **Crater Lake National Park** comprises 400 square miles of alpine meadows, high forest, pumice flats and snow-capped peaks. Within this park, trails lead off in all directions and a 33-mile road encircles the lake. The Pacific Crest Trail is about four miles west of the lake.

ACTIVITIES. Only a few people actually get to the lake. Most folks stand at the rim and respectfully peer down. Those who make the descent must do a steep two-mile round-trip hike.

To tour the lake by boat, get to the north side of the lake via the Cleetwood Trail. Scramble down this substantial drop to the dock. From there, boats take visitors to two islands – the eerie **Phantom Ship** and cone-shaped **Wizard Island**. Fares are $10 for adults, $5.50 for children. Note that, because there are few nutrients in this pure water, fishing is poor.

HIKING. You can take the short loop along the **Castle Crest Wildflower Trail**. Starting from near the Rim Village Information Center, this stroll leads you through masses of summertime wildflowers. The two-mile **Godfrey Glen Trail** begins in the same area and winds down through a verdant valley.

To reach the park's highest point – 8,926 feet – go to the west side of the lake and do the three-mile **Mt. Scott** climb. The hardest hike involves the four-mile walk to the **Pacific Crest Trail**, then to the north on the **Boundary Creek Trail**. This trek, to a source of the Rogue River, is about 10 miles one-way.

ACCOMMODATIONS. Trying to keep the lake's environment free from resort-type development makes overnight facilities rare. The only place right on the lake, is the **Mazama Village Motor Inn**, ☎ 503-594-2511. Built to survive heavy winter snow, the style of this motel is strong and simple. They do have a restaurant and a cocktail lounge. Rates are moderate. Making a reservation ahead of time is suggested.

Some distance away, 25 miles to the north, is a worthwhile destination and a fulcrum for Crater Lake. **Diamond Lake** is a place of beauty, with good fishing and serenity. There is a resort here with both cabins and motel rooms, plus a restaurant. For rates and reservations ☎ 503-793-3333.

Klamath Falls

Population 17,700

Notice on the road map that, after leaving Crater Lake, Highway 97 runs along Klamath Lake for about 20 miles. Klamath Lake is one of the largest bodies of fresh water in Oregon.

This sprawling, usually shallow lake and its associated marshes and wetlands used to be home to millions of migrating ducks, geese and a huge population of cormorants, pelicans and herons. But, because of land reclamation for farming, some of that migratory wildlife disappeared. Fortunately, it seems to be returning. Bird watchers will be in paradise here, with plenty of unusual bird life, including white pelicans with wing spreads of 10 feet and bald eagles.

In the area of Klamath Falls there is a rich history of recent Indian life, including museum artifacts recalling the 19th-century Modoc Indian War, when the U.S. Cavalry was chasing the Modoc Indian named "Captain Jack." Visit the **Favell Museum** in Klamath Falls for this sort of lore.

Klamath Falls is a comfortable, unpretentious place about 18 miles north of the California border. There is, however, one unusual thing about this small city. It has a plentiful supply of naturally heated geothermal water underground. Piped through radiators and grids, this water is used to heat homes, schools, businesses – and it melts the snow from sidewalks.

ACCOMMODATIONS. The three best motels are the **Best Western Olympic Inn**, 2627 S. 6th (☎ 503-882-9665), the **Comfort Inn**, 2500 S. 6th (☎ 503-884-9999) and the **Red Lion Inn**, 3612 S. 6th St. (☎ 800-547-8010). Rates at all three are moderate.

The very well maintained **Oregon Motel** 8, 5225 Highway 97 N. (☎ 503-883-3431) is inexpensive. For a bed and breakfast, try **Thompson's**, 1420 Wild Plum Ct. (☎ 503-882-7938). Rates are moderate. **Molatore's Motor Inn**, 100 Main St. (☎ 503-882-4666) has moderate rates.

DINING. The Chez Nous Restaurant just east of town, (☎ 503-883-8719), serves continental meals. The environment in this re-done residence is a pleasant one. Dinner is moderately priced. It has a good wine selection and a pleasant cocktail lounge.

Fiorella's Italian Restaurant is close in, at 6139 Simmers (☎ 503-882-1878). This is a charming family-owned restaurant with an authentic flavor, serving tasty Italian fare. It has a good wine selection and a cocktail lounge. Dinner is moderately priced.

At least five of the motels have dining room-cocktail lounge facilities.

Eastern Oregon

The term "Eastern Oregon" refers to the largest portion of the state – an area with the deepest canyons, the largest wildlife refuges, the greatest rodeos, extensive deserts (one-quarter of Oregon is desert) and imposing distances between gas stations.

It doesn't really matter how you approach Eastern Oregon. You can get there easily from California, Nevada or Idaho. Heading east from Portland is a good choice. I'll start with that.

The Dalles (see page 60) is a gateway to Eastern Oregon and from there I-84 runs through the desert, along the Columbia River for 130 miles to Pendleton. River views along this route are abundant, there are few trees, and the small desert towns come and go – Biggs, Rufus, Arlington, Boardman. Spaces are wide here and human habitation is sparse.

Pendleton

Population 15,100

Don't come to Pendleton at **Round-Up** time without motel reservations. This big event, held in the second week of September, occupies four days and people come from all over the U.S. During those four days, visitors enter the spirit of the times and folks who

Eastern Oregon

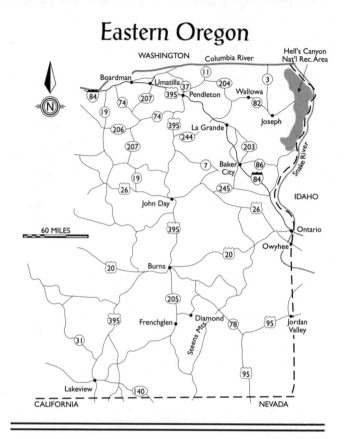

WASHINGTON Columbia River Hell's Canyon Nat'l Rec. Area

N

Boardman
Umatilla (37)
(11)
(204)
(3)
(84)
(74)
(207)
(395) Pendleton
Wallowa
(82)
(19)
(74)
Joseph
(206)
(395) La Grande
(207)
(244)
(203)
(7) Baker City
(86)
(19)
(84)
Snake River
(26)
(245)
IDAHO
John Day
(26)
60 MILES
(395)
Ontario
(20)
Owyhee
(20)
Burns
(20)
(205)
(395) Frenchglen
Diamond
(78)
(95) Jordan Valley
(31)
Steens Mts.
(95)
Lakeview
(140)
CALIFORNIA
NEVADA

have never been on a horse wear boots and cowboy hats. In the evening every bar-restaurant-tavern is filled with lively celebrants.

The rodeo itself is held close to town at the well-marked Round-Up stadium. Tickets sell for $5-$10 per day. There are daily afternoon rodeos that include rodeo stars doing bulldogging, wild horse racing and calf roping. Indian teepee villages inhabited by northwest tribes are on hand. So are parades of stage coaches fully regaled Indians, packtrains and whooping cowboys.

Seen at any other time, Pendleton is a comfortable, friendly, business-like desert town that owes its economic livelihood to widespread, rolling wheat fields, truck gardening and the well-known Woolen Mills. If you pause in Pendleton be sure to take the 1½-hour guided tour of **The Underground Tunnels**. These are downtown and were built under the city streets. You can see the old frontier Shamrock Card Room, the Meat Market, a jail, living quarters for the sequestered Chinese and a once-thriving bordello. Fee for the tour is $5-$10.

THE PENDLETON WOOLEN MILLS. All Northwesterners know about the Woolen Mills as a place they can buy beautifully woven Indian-style blankets, sportswear, perhaps a plaid shirt. The mills are near the Round-Up grounds.

THE ROUND-UP HALL OF FAME. This museum at the Round-Up grounds displays memorabilia, photos and Indian artifacts. Entrance is free.

ACCOMMODATIONS AND DINING. The Best Western Pendleton, off I-84 at exit 210 (☎ 503-276-2135), is nicely appointed, with a pool. Rates are moderate. **The Chaparral Motel,** off I-84 at exit 209, (☎ 503-276-8654), is comfortable and has a dining room. Rates are inexpensive. **The Red Lion Inn,** off I-84 at exit 210, ☎ 503-276-6111, has a restaurant, cocktail lounge and occasional entertainment. Rates are expensive. **The Tapadero Motor Inn,** off I-84 at exit 207, ☎ 503-276-3231, has a dining room-cocktail lounge. Rates are inexpensive.

The animated **Rainbow Bar & Grill** is much-frequented by locals. It's right downtown at 209 S. Main. Popular also is the more sedate **Cimmiyottis** at 137 Main Street. They serve good Italian dishes and have a cocktail lounge.

BEYOND PENDLETON, a scenic stretch of I-84 climbs up and over Blue Mountain Summit and in about 60 miles enters La Grande. Here there is an important junction.

La Grande

Population 11,800

La Grande, supported by fruit, livestock, lumber and recreational activities, is in wooded country, somewhat out of the desert. It lies along the "Oregon Trail" at the foot of the Blue Mountains. Eastern Oregon State College is here as well. More importantly, it's from La Grande that Highway 82 runs north through the Wallowa Mountains, the town of Joseph, and Wallowa Lake to the Hell's Canyon area.

If you arrive in La Grande at the end of the day and you're considering the trip up Highway 82 to Joseph, the Wallowas and beyond, prepare yourself with a layover in this attractive town.

ACCOMMODATIONS AND DINING. The Best Western Pony Soldier Inn, off I-84 at exit 261, ☎ 503-963-7195, with a restaurant nearby, is an attractive motel with moderate rates. **The Broken Arrow Lodge**, 2215 E. Adams Avenue, ☎ 503-963-7116, has a dining room and rates are inexpensive. **The Super 8 Motel**, off I-84 at exit 261, ☎ 505-963-8080, is a nicely equipped place. Some rooms have kitchens, there is a restaurant nearby, and rates are moderate.

The Wrangler Steak House at 1914 Adams Avenue is, as it sounds, a western-style restaurant with frontier decor. They have good, solid American cooking and a salad bar. Prices are moderate. For more stylish dining, step into the **Centennial House**. It has a cocktail lounge and serves well turned out continental food. Moderately expensive. For Mexican food, try **Mamacita's**, 110 Depot St. The food is zesty and good, the bar ambiance lively. Moderate prices.

Leaving La Grande and the freeway, Highway 82 does a 70-mile arc north through pastoral valleys, past canyons and alpine vistas, then across the Grand Ronde River. The road runs through the towns of Elgin, Minam, Longine, Enterprise and finally the town of Joseph, which is near the north end of Wallowa Lake.

A BIT OF HISTORY. Not only is this spectacular country, but history has been made here too. This is the land of Chief Joseph, the elder, and his son. It was the young Chief Joseph, leader of the Nez Perce tribe, whoresponded to the U.S. takeover of their lands (in the 1870's) with stiff resistance and then fled. As Chief Joseph and his followers retreated 1,000 miles, nearly to Canada, they halted often to battle and sometimes overwhelm superior federal troops. But finally, with hunger and exhaustion setting in, they had to surrender. Tragically, their surrender occurred only a few miles from freedom in Canada. Historians agree that Chief Joseph not only put up a good and honorable fight, he demonstrated unusual ability at military tactics. Chief Joseph died in exile, far from his beloved land, in 1904.

Joseph

Population 1,100

This lively little town, well off the beaten track, has a weathered frontier appearance. But, except for its rustic art colony and the bronze sculptures created at **Valley Bronze of Oregon**, it's nearby Lake Wallowa that draws visitors. Still, a bit of time spent in Joseph at the art galleries or the **Wallowa County Museum** will be rewarding. There you can buy bronze castings of mountain animal life or soak up the Nez Perce's admirable culture.

ACCOMMODATIONS AND DINING. The Indian Lodge Motel, 201 S. Main St, ☎ 503-432-2651, is a comfortable place close to the center of town. Rates are inexpensive. To be both fed and housed in a comfortable farm-style environment, try **Chandler's Bed and Breakfast**, 700 S. Main St, ☎ 503-432-9765. Rates are moderate.

For very substantial food and an active bar go to **Cactus Jack's Cowboy Bar**. You can't miss this place; it's right on Main St.

Wallowa Lake

Altitude 5,000 feet

Only a few miles south of Joseph, glacially stunning Wallowa Lake appears. More people – lots of them – come here than to Joseph, and they stay in one of many lodges, campgrounds and chalets that ring this six-mile lake. It's a busy place in the summer. Come equipped with reservations.

ACCOMMODATIONS AND DINING. The Wallowa Lake Lodge, 60060 Wallowa Lake Highway, ☎ 503-432-9821, has a dining room and rates are moderate. **Eagle Cap Chalets**, 59879 Wallowa Lake Highway, ☎ 503-432-4704, has some rooms equipped with kitchens. Rates are moderate.

For **camping**, the **Wallowa Lake State Park** at the south end of the lake has full hook-ups for RV's as well as tent camping. Everything is available there – hiking, fishing boat rentals, showers, fire pits. In the summer, reservations are required. ☎ 503-432-4185.

For no-nonsense, nonalcoholic eating at reasonable prices try **Russells at the Lake**. Good solid American food is served. **The Camas Dining Room** in the Wallawa Lodge is a little more fashionable and a little more expensive. American and Italian food is served, wine and beer too. **Valis Alpine Deli** does German/Hungarian specialties in an appropriate decor. It's moderately priced.

ACTIVITIES NEAR THE LAKE. The Wallowa Lake Tramway at the lake climbs nearly 4,000 feet to the 8,200 foot level of Mt. Howard. This is said to be the longest and highest tram trip in the U.S. Views from the top are unbelievable. You can see into Idaho, the Eagle Cap Wilderness Area and the rim of Hell's Canyon. There is a hiking trail at the top that runs two miles around the crest. The tram is open, weather permitting, from 10am to 4pm, mid-May to mid-September. Fares are $5-$10.

HIKING. Well-shod, hardy hikers can set off from near the bottom of the Tram and climb into the **Eagle Cap Wilderness Area**, a world of high glacial lakes, 10,000-foot peaks, alpine forests and meadows. Fishing up there is productive and will probably supply two meals a day. Go into this area well prepared. Be sure and leave notice of your departure at the trailhead.

For pack animal assistance, both horses and llamas, perhaps with a guide, contact **Wallowa Llamas**, Rt. 1, Box 84, Halfway OR 97834, ☎ 503-742-2961. Llamas are the coming thing in pack animal travel. They're sure-footed and intelligent, but can carry only a portion of the camper's gear. Ask for current prices.

Traditional pack horse trekking (horses can carry much more weight than llamas) are available at the **Eagle Cap Wilderness Area** Station, Box 241 Joseph, OR 97846, ☎ 503-432-4145. Either of these outfitters can provide trips by the day or by the hour.

The Hell's Canyon
National Recreation Area

From Joseph, there is a paved road that runs northeast for 28 miles to Imnaha. Fill up with gas before leaving Joseph, then proceed through grazing lands, semi-desert, through creek-fed canyons to Imnaha. Here, other than a country store with associated bar and restaurant, there are few amenities and no gasoline.

From Imnaha the going gets rough. It's 24 bumpy, unpaved, top-of-the world miles to **Hat Point**. Plan on two hours one-way to do this trip.

The reason folks go to so much trouble to get to Hat Point is for the grandeur of time-worn smooth slopes, the feeling of uncluttered space and for a view of the Snake River. Standing at the view point of the Hat Point Canyon rim, you look down more than a mile at the serpentine, canyon-bound Snake River.

HELL'S CANYON FLOAT TRIPS. To get on the river for float trips you have to go to the Hell's Canyon Dam. To do this, several routes are available. One is from La Grande along Highway 203 to Medical Springs, on to Halfway, then to Oxbow Dam. Hell's Canyon Dam is 23 miles downriver from Oxbow Dam. Another route is from La Grande along I-84 to Baker, then head east and north to Hell's Canyon Dam. All road maps will show these routes and the mileage in detail.

Hell's Canyon Dam is where most river trips begin. From here, there are jet boats that leave several times a day for two-hour runs. They provide a good sampling of the river. Plan on $25 for adults and $10 for children.

There are more than 30 outfitters who offer float and jet boat trips on the Snake. Count on roughly $50 a day for raft trips. For starters contact **Hell's Canyon Adventure Inc.**, Box 159 Oxbow, Oregon 97840. ☎ 800-422-3568. For a more complete list write **The Supervisor, Hell's Canyon National Recreation Area**, 2535 Riverside Dr., P.O. Box 699, C1arkston, Washington 99403.

Baker City

Population 9,100
Altitude 3,446 feet

I hadn't been in Baker since the late 30's when my father took me with him on a business trip. At that time we stayed at the comfortable 10-story Baker Hotel – an Eastern Oregon skyscraper – and as we left the next day, the day Carol Lombard died in the air crash, my father asked if I'd turned the room lights off. I hadn't. We left anyway.

Last year I returned to Baker and driving into town I caught sight of the now abandoned, time-worn Baker Hotel and in the gathering dusk I saw a solitary light on in one of the upper rooms.

Baker, an 1861 Gold Rush center, is now a pleasantly thriving commercial center for agriculture. More importantly, for visitors interested in the historic "Oregon Trail," Baker is of utmost importance.

The National Historic Oregon Trail Interpretive Center

This center is just out of town, five miles east of the junction of I-84 and Highway 86. There, at the top of Flagstaff Hill, the large Interpretive Center vividly illustrates history and displays artifacts of the Oregon Trail journey. Local volunteers dressed in 1840's costume demonstrate pioneer arts and skills. Stage presentations performed in an amphitheater portray how the 300,000 men, women and children crossed 2,000 miles of American wilderness and how they gambled, won and lost on reaching their destination before winter snow flew. The Baker area was on that route, as shown by portions of a still-visible trail, complete with ruts from the oxen-pulled wagons.

Around the Interpretive Center there are several miles of trails that expose visitors to the sights and sounds encountered by the pioneers on the sagebrushed plains. The center is open 9-6 daily, March-October. Admission is free. It's worth the trip from Portland.

In town be sure and see the **Oregon Trail Regional Museum**. It has a fine collection of rocks, minerals, precious stones, and period clothing and utensils of the 1840's. Admission is $1.50.

Ask in town about the departure of the **Sumpter Valley Railroad**, which carries passengers on a five-mile loop through the historic gold mining areas of Baker. Fee is $4-8; Visit the **U.S. National Bank** at 2000 Main St. and see the 80.4-ounce Armstrong gold nugget found in 1913.

Accommodations & Dining

For eastern Oregon, Baker has an unusually large selection of motels – at least 14 of them.

The Best Western Sun Ridge Inn, Sunridge Lane, ☎ 800-233-2368, has everything – good restaurant, lounge, spa, pool. Rates are moderate. **The A'Demain Bed & Breakfast**, 1790 4th St., ☎ 503-523-2509, is in a restored Victorian house. They offer meals too. All rates are moderate. The comfortable but modest **Friendship Inn**, 134 Bridge Street, ☎ 503-523-6571, is inexpensive. **The Quality Inn**, 810 Campbell St., ☎ 503-523-2242, is pleasant and has a complimentary continental breakfast. Rates are inexpensive. **The Oregon Trail Motel** and Restaurant, 211 Bridge St., ☎ 503-523-5844, is inexpensive.

For affordable, flavorful Mexican food, try the **Burrito Construction Company**, 2nd and Broadway. **The Brass Parrot**, only slightly more expensive, serves Mexican and North American food in a nice historic setting. For Chinese food, walk into **Jimmy Chan's Restaurant** at 1841 Main St. American food is available too. It's inexpensive.

Generally parallel to the Oregon Trail, I-84 runs uneventfully about 80 miles to Ontario. Ontario was the beginning of the Oregon section of the Trail.

Ontario

Population 9,400
Altitude 2,240 feet

Ontario, on the banks of the Snake River, is as far as you can go in Oregon. Portland is 374 miles away and Idaho begins just the other side of the I-84 bridge.

Rather than being a prime tourist destination, Ontario is a functional town complete with a community college and an outstanding medical center. It supports itself nicely on "agri-business." This is the term that applies to growing crops, raising cattle, processing the results, and shipping them. Many of the residents are Mexican-American. They make up the bulk of the manual labor force.

Cattle ranching in Ontario's Malheur County produces huge quantities of beef. Onions, vast fields of them (in August you can smell them before seeing them) are grown here. So are potatoes, sugar beets, corn, peppermint, dairy products, wheat and grain. Better yet, it's here that these products are frozen, processed, packaged and shipped. This is a major trucking center.

As to the recent history of Ontario's Malheur County, it was here during WW II that several thousand Japanese-Americans lost their civil rights and were forced into Relocation Camps. It was a sad page of American history. Still, something came from those unfortunate days. Many of those Japanese who started with nothing remained. Today they are an essential part of this community.

Accommodations & Dining

There are plenty of places to stay and to eat in Ontario. Most are close to the city center.

The Holiday Motel, 615 East Idaho, ☎ 503-889-9188; has nice units and a restaurant with cocktail lounge. Inexpensive. **Howard Johnson Lodge**, 1249 Tapadero Ave., ☎ 503-889-8621, is an attractive motel with a good restaurant and cocktail lounge. Moderate. **Best Western Inn**, 251 Goodfellow St., ☎ 503-889-2600, is a fine place to stay. A restaurant is nearby. Moderate. **Super 8 Hotel**, 266 Goodfellow St., ☎ 507-889-8282, offers nicely furnished rooms. It has a pool, exercise room and nearby restaurant.

Southeastern Oregon

Southeastern Oregon is one of the most dramatically remote areas in the country. There are lonely high deserts inhabited by jack rabbits, rattle snakes, coyotes and herds of wild horses. There are immense lakes – dry, watery or laced with bubbling hotsprings. There are bird refuges where millions of migratory birds gather to feed and rest and, at Hart Mountain near Lakeview, there are immense herds of big horn sheep, prong horn antelope and mule deer. There is adventure to be found in this part of Oregon. However, a few cautionary words are in order.

Winter in this region can be severe and roads are often impassable. Approach winter travel with respect.

In summer it can be very hot, very dry. Go equipped with plenty of water, food and matches. Don't leave established roads. If you get stuck or break down don't abandon the car and attempt to walk out. Wait for help in the shade of the car – not in it. Be sure the car is in good condition and, of course, gassed up. Enter this part of Oregon by driving south from Ontario on Highway 201. At the town of Owyhee, turn right and follow signs to Owyhee Dam and its lake. It's about 15 miles from Owyhee.

Owyhee Dam & The Lake

Hemmed in by multicolored cliffs, this lake is surrounded by harsh desert terrain and is part of the important Owyhee Irrigation System.

Fishing is good here, for bass, crappies and trout. There is a boat ramp at the lake as well as a good campsite for RV hook-ups.

Succor Creek State Park

Retrace your route back to Highway 201 and continue south into the Succor Creek Canyon. Scenery here, along what used to be a stage coach route, is eerie, dry and abrupt. At the Recreation Center there is a campground by the creek.

Jordan Valley

Population 400

Jordan Valley is 85 miles south of Ontario. You're now in a lone-some part of Oregon and a tidy little town founded by Basque sheepherders in the 1890's.

Once, on my way to Winnemucca, Nevada, I pulled into Jordan Valley, tired and hungry at the end of the day. I checked into the comfortable **Sahara Motel** – rates are inexpensive. When restored, I dined sumptuously at **The Basque Restaurant**. You can't miss it. The meal, lamb, chicken, hearty bean soup laced with onions and tomatoes, pasta, a salad, all washed down with house wine, was worth the trip alone. Then, next morning, as I gassed up at the sole station, the attendant gave me a pair of $5 gambling coupons for use in Winnemucca. I wish I could say I won a fortune with them.

Rome

Population – tiny

Heading west across the desert on Highway 95, the hamlet of Rome appears. This farm community on the banks of the Owyhee

River is the put-in site for rafts running the tempestuous Owyhee River Canyons. This trip is done only in April and May. In high summer there's not enough water.

Rafters who do this trip experience all the solitude of the high desert. They'll soak in natural hot springs and explore ancient Indian sites. The trips are for either four or nine days and outfitters request that only whitewater veterans apply. For rates and information, write: **White Water Adventures**, P.O. Box 249, Cresswell, OR 97426. ☎ 800-289-4534.

From Rome, desert-bound Highway 95 goes to Burns Junction, about 10 miles. Here the road forks and Highway 95 goes its lonesome way south to the Nevada border and eventually on to Winnemucca.

Going northwest from Burns Junction, Highway 78 moves across the desert, over 5,085-foot Duck Pond Ridge Summit and, after about 100 miles, enters Burns.

Burns

Population 2,900
Altitude 4,148 feet

Burns, with its neighbor Hines, is in Oregon's largest county (Harney), and it may be one of the most "away-from-it-all" towns in the country.

With a legacy of 19th-century cattle barons who acquired a million acres of high desert grazing ground and ran herds of cattle, this is still a genuine cowboy town. Without any tourist gimmickry, Burns makes few claims to urban beauty. It caters to what is necessary: food, clothing, cattleman supplies, building material, a lively tavern or two and some card rooms. Burns is a friendly, hospitable haven.

Accommodations & Dining

The Orbit Hotel, 1½ mile north of Burns, is classified as a luxury-budget motel. A restaurant is next door. (☎ 800-235-6155). **The Royal Inn**, 999 Oregon Ave., ☎ 503-573-5295, has an indoor swimming pool, sauna and spa. There is a restaurant close by. Inexpensive. **The Silver Spur Motel**, 789 N. Broadway, ☎ 503-573-2077, is very comfortable and is inexpensive.

The Pine Room Café, on Monroe St. in town, is one of my favorites. They serve good solid American and German food and lots of home-baked fresh bread. Prices are modest. For a little congenial western bar fun, followed by hearty western fare – steaks, prime ribs, chicken and homemade pies – try **The Powerhouse** on Monroe St. Prices are modest.

From Burns

Travelers can proceed west along Highway 20 for about 130 miles to Bend. Along this desert run, the road passes through the "oasis towns" of Riley, Hampton, Brothers, Millican, lonely little settlements with a gas station, maybe a simple restaurant and always friendly helpful people.

But for the ultimate in backroad adventure, the 200-mile scenic byway from Burns to Lakeview is highly recommended. To do this trip, take Highway 205 south. This leads to **Wrights Points**, a good area for agate hunting about 20 miles south of Burns. Next, about 30 miles south of Burns, the road passes across a neck of water separating Harney Lake from Malheur Lake. Both of these huge, marshy lakes, surrounded by arid desert, are host to thousands of birds and waterfowl: mallards, teal, pelican, Canadian geese and hundreds of other species. They draw bird watchers from all over. Bring binoculars.

For further background, drive east on an unpaved road, from the southern edge of the lake's neck to New Princeton, roughly 10 miles. Here there is a museum and information center.

Diamond Valley

About 15 miles south of the lake, a side road goes east to the Diamond Craters, which are the domed pillars and pits left by ancient volcanic activity. While on this 20-mile loop road, visit the famous corral called the "Round Barn." This old structure was built by rancher Pete French to break saddle horses.

The Steens Mountains

Back on Highway 205, continue south toward Frenchglen. From Frenchglen turn east and do the 60-mile loop into the Steens Mountains. Check locally about this road, which is open from mid-July to late October. If your car does not have high clearance, avoid this trip.

Leaving Frenchglen, the road climbs gradually, deceptively (the highest point is 9,670 feet) and the desert is left below. Pines begin to appear, as do meadows bordered by aspens and framed by clear, trout-filled streams. Eventually the road – such as it is – fetches up at the summit. Below, to the east, you can see the grim Alvord Desert. There are camping spots along this loop – Lily Lake, Fish Lake and Page Springs. Return to Highway 205 about 10 miles south of Frenchglen.

Frenchglen

Population – the fingers of both hands

Frenchglen, which looks like the setting for a western movie, was named after the flamboyant, controversial cattle baron, Pete French. If you're low on gas, tired or hungry you'll be glad to enter Frenchglen. It has a store, gas pump, a small restaurant and a campsite called **Steens Mountain Resort** with 24 spaces (☎ 503-493-2415). More importantly, this is the location of the famed **Frenchglen Hotel** and Dining Room. It's now classified as an historic state park.

Do not come here without reservations made well in advance. ☎ 503-493-2825. They're open from March to November. Rooms are simple, food is family-style and excellent. Moderate.

Hart Mountain National Antelope Refuge

Continuing south on Highway 205, the paved road lasts another seven miles. Here you turn west on a gravel road, Harney County Road 412. This leads on about 50 miles to the Hart Mountain Refuge. The Refuge Headquarters is about 15 miles from the east boundary.

The Refuge itself occupies 275,000 acres of high plateau country above a series of marshy lakes to the west. There is a primitive campground in the area and near the Visitors Center is a pleasant and usable hot spring.

Hart Mountain is home to the well-protected prong horn antelope. There are thousands of them, but they are not always easy to see – nor are the resident bighorn sheep. Still, you'll see jackrabbits by the score, usually mule deer and a wide selection of bird life.

From Hart Mountain, the road forges steeply down to the west and passes through the Warner Wetlands. This is another good place to see migrating waterfowl.

At the farming village of Plush, with a welcome gas station and shaded by cottonwoods and poplars, the road becomes paved. Then, 19 miles beyond Plush, the road intersects with Highway 140, followed by Highway 395. After 20 miles it enters Lakeview.

Lakeview

Population 2,500
Altitude 4,800 feet

Lakeview, the county seat of Lake County, is one of Oregon's highest towns. It's on Highway 395 just 15 miles north of the California border. It's a good through-route for traveling south to either Reno or San Francisco.

This small town, with its downtown vintage brick buildings, is a marketing-shipping center for surrounding cattle ranches. And, with cattle in mind, a rodeo is held in Lakeview during Labor Day weekend. To look at Lakeview's pioneer past and see relics of those days, visit the **Schminck Memorial Museum** at 128 South E St. Ten miles N.E. of town, there is winter skiing at the **Warner Canyon Ski Area**. Native plants and wildlife can be seen right in town along the **Lakeview Nature Trail**.

ACCOMMODATIONS AND DINING. The Best Western Sky-line Motor Lodge, 414 North G St, ☎ 800-528-1234, has a pool, whirlpool and serves continental breakfast. Moderate. **The Interstate 8 Motel**, 354 North K St, ☎ 503-947-3341, has a restaurant. Inexpensive.

Hunter's RV Park, Highway 395 North, ☎ 503-947-4968, has 23 spaces. Inexpensive.

For simple, inexpensive but good American food, step into the **Indian Village**, 1st and E St. The **Shamrock Café**, at E and 2nd St., offers similar food. For Chinese-American food, go to **King's Café**, 1st and F St.

To return directly to Central Oregon, eventually to Portland, 338 miles away, go north on Highway 395 for 23 miles to Valley Falls. Turn west on Highway 31 and follow what is known as the Fremont Highway to La Pine, about 120 miles. This road was named after General Fremont who, as a young officer-explorer in 1843, led his men over this route.

This is lonesome country, but not quite raw desert. Sagebrush mixed with clumps of yellow pine, green meadows and agricultural land softens the scenery. Then there are the lakes, Summer and Silver, shallow, marshy, filled with waterfowl and with wisps of steam rising into the air from underground hot springs. Going north from La Pine, all roads lead to Portland.

But to finish off Eastern Oregon in style, continue north from Lakeview along Highway 395, through the desert, across alkali flats, past the oasis of Wagontire to Riley – 114 miles. At Riley, travel east on Highway 20 for the 28-mile return to Burns. From Burns continue due north on Highway 395 for 70 miles. Forests of ponderosa pine appear, then the 5,152-foot pass of Canyon Summit. Finally, the road enters the towns of Canyon City and John Day.

John Day - Canyon City

Combined Population 2,400
Altitude 3,083 feet

Canyon City, with its 600 people, is the county seat of Grant County. Its larger neighbor, John Day is the business trading center for cattle, logging and agriculture.

Lying in a broad valley surrounded by the rugged mountains of the Malheur National Forest, John Day was named after a young man who was part of an errant, often-lost scouting expedition sent out by John Jacob Astor in 1811. Then, during the Gold Rush years of 1862-64, Canyon City and John Day were on the pony express route to The Dalles.

The **Kam Wah Chung Museum** in John Day, next to the City Park, is set in what was a Chinese doctor's office and store. There are displays of more than 1,000 Chinese and western medicines used by herbal doctors. Old records and relics are also on view. Admission is $2.

In Canyon City, the **Grant County Historical Museum** houses relics of explorers, Indians, and the Gold Rush. Admission is $2. Then, for a pilgrimage to the home of Oregon's poet, enter **Joaquin Miller's Cabin**, next door to the museum. Some of the poems written by this earthy, dashing pony express rider, traveler and raconteur are on display in the cabin. Joaquin Miller's real name was Cincinnatus Heine but, in honor of the California-Mexican bandit, Joaquin Murietta, he changed his name to Joaquin Miller.

ACCOMMODATIONS AND DINING. The Budget 8 Motel, 711 W. Main St., ☎ 503-575-2155, is comfortable and inexpensive. **The Best Western Inn**, 315 S.W. Main St., ☎ 503-375-1700, is a well-kept motel. Rates are moderate. **The Dreamers Lodge**, 144 N. Canyon Blvd., ☎ 503-575-0526, is comfortable and inexpensive. There is a restaurant nearby.

Annie Ann's Café and Lounge in Canyon City is an older but friendly western-style café serving good solid American food. Prices are modest. The **Grubsteak Mining Company** and the **Mother Lode Restaurant**, both on John Day's Main Street, are places for hearty western dining.

Alcohol is served at the Grubsteak, but not at the Mother Lode.

Going west from John Day along Highway 26, the road follows the John Day River through wooded farming country and through the tiny towns of Mt. Vernon and Dayville for 32 miles. About this time, things get more interesting and a narrow canyon with the river at its bottom leads on to the **John Day Fossil Beds National Monument**. This area is near the junction of Highway 26 and Highway 19.

Comprising 14,000 acres, the Monument has sections that display colorful fossil-bearing formations. Fossil collecting is strictly prohibited, but the hiking, picnicking and fishing in the John Day River makes it very worthwhile. Wildflowers in this area are spectacular and there is camping at the Monument Park.

Continue west on Highway 26 from the Fossil Beds and, in roughly 80 miles, you'll have gone through the Ochoco National Forest and entered Prineville, both discussed above.

From Prineville it's a straight shot of 146 miles, via Madras, Warm Springs and Mt. Hood, to Portland. At this point you've closed an immense circle and are poised to enter Washington State.

Washington

Population 4,866,700
Area 56,511 square miles.
Capital Olympia.
Highest Point Mt. Rainier, 14,410 feet.
Admitted to the Union 1889

Like Oregon, Washington has its forested, lush and green western parts. As in Oregon, the Cascade Range runs from north to south, separating verdant western areas from the broad sagebrush plains and rolling wheat producing country. You can't drive very far in Washington without seeing signs indicating a park, a campsite or a historical marker.

But Washington's western topography is more complex and the coast is interrupted by bays, inlets and what nearly amounts to an inland sea – Puget Sound.

Regions of Washington

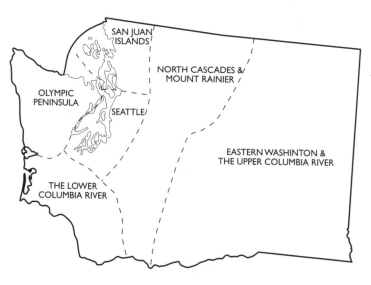

Washington's economy is extremely diverse. Farmland occupies about 40% of the state's area, stretches of land with orchards, wheatfields, truck gardens, dairies, cattle farms and an ever-growing system of vineyards, second only to California.

Catching, processing, and shipping of fish and shellfish is a major industry. Then there is aircraft and transportation equipment manufacturing (as in Boeing), shipbuilding, and Microsoft, the huge software company.

Most travelers will probably begin with an entrance from Oregon along I-5 towards Seattle. Or they will come in by plane at Sea-Tac International Airport, which is halfway between Seattle and Tacoma on Highway 99. We will explore the state by regions in the following order. 1. The Lower Columbia River. 2. Seattle and its approach via I-5. 3. The San Juan Islands. 4. The Olympic Peninsula. 5. The Northern Cascades and Mt. Rainier. 6. Eastern Washington and the Upper Columbia River.

The Lower Columbia River

According to my Portland, Oregon grandparents, going to the seashore (when the century was young) was done for a month or more, rather than for the weekend. In those days, Long Beach, Washington was a favorite destination – chosen, I suspect, for its convenience. Roads weren't that good, nor was the automobile.

They would board a river boat in the evening and sail the hundred miles downriver to a point near the mouth of the Columbia River. The river steamer, *Georgianna*, was a stylish favorite for travelers. Passengers would dance to an orchestra, dinner would be served in the salon and in due time folks would nod off in comfortable cabins. The next morning, passengers would step off the boat and board a train for the short run to Long Beach and beyond.

In Long Beach, and all along the 28-mile peninsula (a mile wide) that dead-ended at the mouth of Willapa Bay, there were hotels, inns, guest houses and fine places to eat. Visitors strolled the wide sandy beaches, rode bicycles, played croquet, ate well and breathed the bracing Pacific Ocean air.

The Lower Columbia River

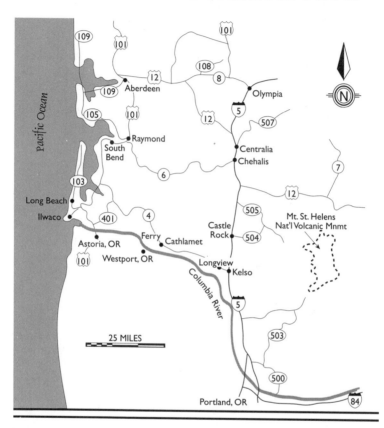

If such a method of transportation still existed, I would be first in line to buy tickets, as would legions of others who appreciate the virtues of leisurely travel.

Getting to the Long Beach Peninsula is now much faster. From Portland, this trip is best done by driving to Astoria and crossing the 4.1-mile toll bridge to the Washington side. From there, veer left from Highway 101 to Highway 103 and drive to Fort Canby, where there are sites for RV hook-ups, picnicking and general camping. Fishing from the nearby jetty is good, as are views of the mouth of the Columbia River. Continue from there only two miles to Ilwaco.

Ilwaco

Population 800

This little town at the southern end of the Long Beach peninsula is known as the "graveyard of the Pacific." Here there is a treacherous sand bar that is the scene of many shipwrecks. In good weather, charter boat fishing from Ilwaco is very good.

Cape Disappointment, with its historic lighthouse, is four miles south of Ilwaco. This is a good place for lively, blustery views of the Columbia River's mouth. Lewis and Clark were here in the winter of 1805. They were not enchanted with the violent winter storms they endured at Cape Disappointment.

Long Beach

Population 1,200 – many more in summer

This community and its neighbors to the north – Klipsan Beach, Ocean Park, Nahcotta and Oysterville – are all resort towns. They've all got camper parks, a series of motels and restaurants that range from passable to superb, and long wide stretches of beach.

In Long Beach, as in some of the other communities, a few of the buildings remain that my grandparents would recognize, including a boardwalk that runs along 2,300 feet of beachfront.

People these days come to this area for razor clam digging, salmon fishing, oyster eating, to play golf and to walk on the flat sandy beaches. I'm sorry to add that motorists drive, often with abandon, on the beaches.

Near Long Beach, visit **The Clarke Rhododendron Nursery**. For viewing azaleas and rhododendrons, the best time is in May.

For those who are into kites, the **World Kite Museum** displays more than 600 kites from around the world. This is also popular kite flying country.

CLAMMING. Razor clams are particularly abundant along this 28-mile-long peninsula. They are found in the usual way, by spotting the small hole they leave in the sand. Then the clammer digs quickly and tries not to cut into the clam. A razor clam can burrow over a foot a minute.

CRABBING. In Nahcotta, 11 miles north of Long Beach, crabbing can be done in rental boats, with rings provided. This takes place on Willapa Bay, but you should keep one eye on the tide. Being stranded in mud flats at low tide could involve a long, cold wait.

OYSTERS. This important industry is centered in Willapa Bay and is the source of very fine, nationally famous oysters. Gathering oysters on your own is not allowed, but they can be bought nearly anywhere, particularly in Nahcotta or Oysterville.

Finally, at the north end of the peninsula, a fine place for beach-dune walking, is **Leadbetter Point State Park**.

Accommodations & Dining

The Anchorage Motor Court is one mile north of town on Highway 103 (☎ 360-642-2351). This pleasant motel has ocean-view rooms. Rates are moderate. **Nendel's Edgewater Inn**, a quarter-mile south of town (☎ 360-542-2311), is a very nice motel with many ocean-view rooms and a dining room. Rates are moderate. **Our Place at the Beach** is at the south end of town (☎ 360-642-3793); inexpensive. The **Shaman Hotel**, downtown (☎ 360-642-3714), has ocean-view rooms, with a restaurant nearby. Rates are moderate. **Super 8 Motel**, downtown, is on the beach (☎ 360-642-8988). Rates are moderate.

The Lightship Restaurant, at Nendel's Edgewater Inn, has a cocktail lounge. It's a very popular restaurant serving well-prepared, healthy meals. Dinner is moderately priced. **The Milton York**, right downtown, serves both seafood and conventional cooking. Good breakfasts are served there. Dinner is inexpensive. In Nahcotta on Nahcotta Dock, overlooking Willapa Bay, **The Ark** is popular, with its cocktail lounge and fine seafood. Dinner is moderate.

There are plenty of smaller restaurants, from the fast-food variety to little seafood cafés where local shellfish and seafood are served.

From Long Beach

Going east up the Columbia River from the Long Beach area, it's best to cross the bridge back into Astoria and take Highway 30 towards Portland. As mentioned earlier, the ferry from Westport, Oregon across to Cathlamet on the Washington side is a most delightful way to travel this section.

Cathlamet

Population 500

Cathlamet, a picturesque riverside town with strong Scandinavian roots, is the site of an unusually good historic bed and breakfast getaway. The **Country Keeper B&B, Bradley House** is on Main Street, ☎ 360-795-3030. Overlooking Puget Island and the Columbia River, this resplendent Victorian home, without the distractions of either TV or phones, is worth looking into. Rates are moderate.

Longview - Kelso

Combined population 42,500

These twin cities are logging-milling-shipping ports where ships from all over the world carry away Northwest wood products. They are also a fishing and canning center. This is where travelers join I-5 for a direct run to Seattle.

In both Kelso and Longview there are an abundance of motels, most in plain view when entering or leaving the area. Unfortunately, as filled with amenities as these twin cities are, it may be too soon after either Portland or Long Beach to pause for more than a good meal.

Mt. St. Helens

Elevation 8,365 feet

A pair of my best summers, ever, circa 1933-34, were spent at a YMCA Camp at the foot of Mt. St. Helens, alongside clear, cold and magnificent Spirit Lake. There, directed by college-age counselors, we took four to five day hikes into the alpine vastness of the Cascades, we perfected our maritime skills while whale-boat rowing on the large gin-clear lakes and climaxed the summer with an ascent of Mt. St. Helens. It then had an elevation of 9,665 feet.

I remember that on the eve of that climb, we camped at Timberline on the flank of the mountain and began our climb at first light. I recall our guide pausing reverently before we set out that florid morning, to ask the mountain's permission for our ascent. For a 13-year-old, this was heady stuff.

Mt. St. Helens isn't 9,665 feet high anymore. The eruption of May 1980 removed 1,300 feet of the mountain and turned pristine Spirit Lake into a mud hole. It also choked adjacent rivers, wiped out trout-bearing streams, devastated forests for miles and sent clouds of ash around the world. Fortunately for major centers of population like Portland, Seattle and Vancouver B.C., prevailing winds blew malevolent clouds of ash in a different direction.

Still, nature heals itself and today new trees are growing, streams are returning to life and, perhaps someday, the magnificence that was Spirit Lake will return.

To see what the powers of nature can do, both positive and negative, drive north on I-5 to exit 49 (near Castle Rock, about 49 miles from the Oregon-Washington border). Continue five miles eastward and visit the **Mt. St. Helens National Volcanic Monument Visitors Center.** They have films and models that detail the explosion and its aftermath. Close by, roads – some unpaved – lead into the volcanic area. Here you can see and feel the powers of nature.

Seattle & Its Approach By I-5

Continue north through peaceful woods and fields of agriculture, past Chehalis and Centralia, to Washington's capital, Olympia.

Olympia

Population 33,900

Olympia has what is known as the "capitol group," the government buildings. This area is set into 55 beautiful acres of classic landscaping. There are cherry blossoms in the spring, flamboyant

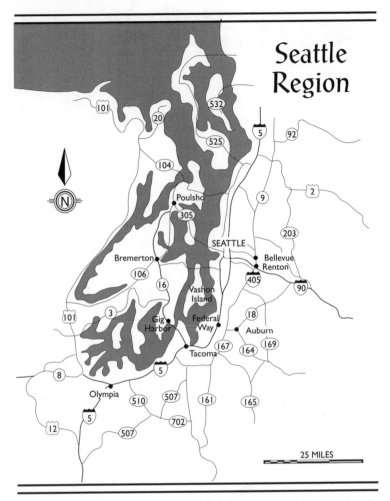

Seattle
Region

rhododendrons soon after and several greenhouses – open to the public – that nourish this impressive flora.

Nearby at the **State Capital Museum**, 211 W. 21st Ave., is an Italian Renaissance mansion that houses artifacts, documents and photos displaying Washington's early history, including the Northwest Coast Indians. Admission is $2.

Very prominent, popular too, is the **Olympic Brewing Co**. This is in the neighboring town of Tumwater, which is just off I-5 at exit 103. This brewery, a division of the Pabst Brewing Company, offers tours to taste the product and see how it is made. Admission is free. Open daily.

Geographically speaking, an important junction occurs at Olympia. An easy way to reach the Olympic Peninsula is by turning left off I-5 and following Highway 101 north. This route runs past Hoods Canal, the western arm of Puget Sound and continues up and around the top of the Olympic Peninsula. This is a good choice, one I'll cover later.

Near Olympia

What goes on in this, the southernmost part of Puget Sound, is important for several reasons. One is that some of the people who cruise and sail Puget Sound say they prefer this many-armed, many-islanded bit of inland sea to the northern areas – including the San Juan Islands. Not all sailors agree but, to pursue boating in this area, consult the yellow pages under "Boat Renting."

OYSTERS. Oyster lovers will be locally informed that the famous Olympia Oyster, beloved among gourmets, is farmed in the beds of South Puget Sound – places like Mud, Oyster, Big and Little Skookum Bays. The largest oyster beds are at the Olympia Oyster Co., which is off Highway 101 north of Olympia. Visitors are welcome.

ACCOMMODATIONS AND DINING. The Best Western Aladdin Motor Inn, downtown off I-5 at exit 105, ☎ 360-352-7200, is near the State Capitol. It has all amenities, including a dining room and cocktail lounge. Rates are moderate. **The Quality Inn Westwater**, off I-5 at exit 104, ☎ 360-943-4000, is in an attractive setting overlooking Capitol Lake and the Capitol Dome. It has a dining room and cocktail lounge. Rates are moderate. **The Ramada Inn-Governor House**, downtown at 621 S. Capital Way, has a dining room, cocktail lounge and entertainment. Rates are moderate. **The Golden Gavel**, off I-5 at exit 105B, ☎ 360-352-8531, with restaurant nearby, is a comfortable choice. Rates are inexpensive. A bed and breakfast, the historic **Harbinger House**, off I-5 at City Center exit, has moderate rates.

Ben Moore's Restaurant, at 112 W. 4th Ave., serves American food, cocktails too, in a pleasantly casual dining room. Dinners are moderately priced. For seafood try **Geonas** on the Bay, 1525 N. Washington. Dinners are moderately priced.

FROM OLYMPIA. Up I-5 from Olympia to Seattle (60 miles), traffic picks up, approaching Southern California standards.

Towns, highway junctions, military bases, airports lie cheek by jowl, all of them contributing to urban congestion.

Ft. Lewis

A working army base covering many acres of this green land appears 18 miles northeast of Olympia. For military history buffs, there is an exceptional **military museum** just off I-5 at exit 120. Admission is free.

Tacoma

Population 176,700

The name Tacoma is derived from the Puyallup Indian name for what we know as Mt. Rainier, "Tahoma." The third largest city in Washington, Tacoma is not only an important deep water port on the southern end of Puget Sound, but it is also a major junction for northbound travelers looking to avoid the traffic of I-5 and approach Seattle in a more dramatic way. It is here that, by turning west from I-5 onto Highway 16, they can proceed north via the Narrows Bridge to the Kitsap Peninsula. This area, laced with bays, close to Hood Canal and the western part of Puget Sound, provides a more interesting approach to Seattle.

Using Highway 16 from Tacoma to Bremerton – about 30 miles – you can take a very good ferry trip from Bremerton to Seattle. This is worth serious consideration. But Tacoma first.

Coming up I-5 from the south, all Tacoma becomes suddenly visible – particularly the prominent Tacoma Sports Dome. Pause if you like in this very livable city, a center for the wood products industry and for shipping activities. Visit the public fishing pier at Ruston Way near **Point Defiance Park**. This is north of Highway 16 in North Tacoma. Spend some time at this park, which has 700 acres of green beauty, including footpaths that provide scenic views of the sound. Boat rentals with fishing gear are available there plus a zoo and aquarium with displays of all the marine life in Puget Sound.

If your timing is right, take in a Seattle Sonics or Tacoma Rockets hockey match at the **Tacoma Sports Dome**. For information about other events in the Dome, call the ticket office ☎ 206-572-3663.

Spend some time shopping, wandering, and eating in "old town" Tacoma at McCarver St. and Ruston Way in north Tacoma. See one of the tallest totem poles in the nation. Carved from a single cedar tree, this totem pole is 105 feet high. This is at Fireman's Park, at the end of S. Ninth St.

ACCOMMODATIONS AND DINING. Best thing to do is stay on I-5 when entering or leaving town. Motels become very obvious. A good choice, with a restaurant, is the **Best Western Lakewood Motor Inn**, which is off I-5 at exit 125 (☎ 206-584-2212). Rates are moderate. To stay downtown, try the **Sheraton Tacoma Hotel**, which has all amenities, including convention facilities, free parking, cocktail lounge and dining room (☎ 206-572-3200). Expensive. **The Shiloh Inn**, off I-5 at northbound exit 128, with a restaurant nearby, is comfortable, with moderate rates. **The Sherwood Inn**, with restaurant and lounge, is referred to as "The Tacoma Landmark" and is off I-5 at northbound exit 128S. It has a restaurant and lounge. Rates are inexpensive (☎ 206-535-2800). **The EconoLodge**, off I-5 at exit 127, says "Spend a night – not a fortune." A restaurant is near. Inexpensive. ☎ 206-582-7550. There are plenty of other choices, most in plain sight.

For seafood dining in town try **Johnny's Dock**, off I-5 at exit 133, near the Dome. Dinner is moderately priced. **Stanley and Seaforts** has traditional seafood and steaks, overlooking the city and Commencement Bay. It's near exit 133 off I-5. Dinners are moderately priced.

For Italian meals, try the **Olive Garden**, off I-5 at northbound exit 128, or the popular family restaurant, **Old Spaghetti Factory**, downtown near the depot. Dinners at both places are inexpensive. For sophisticated dining, continental style, **The Cliff House** at 6300 Marine View Drive, near exit 142B off I-5, has good views and fine food with a northwest influence. Dinner is expensive. For American food, buffet-style, the **Old Country Buffet** is very good and inexpensive. The address is 10121 Gravelly Lake Drive, off I-5 at exit 125.

As in any city the size of Tacoma, restaurants of every persuasion are plentiful and obvious.

FROM TACOMA. A very worthwhile alternate route to Seattle takes you via I-5 in Tacoma onto Highway 16, then northwest across the Narrows Bridge to the Kitsap Peninsula. The Narrows

Bridge, 2,800 feet long, replaces an earlier bridge that made the news in 1940. The original bridge, an "architectural failure," was dubbed "galloping Gertie" for the way it pitched, swayed and finally collapsed shortly after its opening in 1940.

Gig Harbor

Population 3,200

This small town, a fashionable community in an arm of Puget Sound, is a very good address indeed. It's filled with woodsy upper-scale homes and by the water there are shops, good restaurants and bait basins. But, unless you are interested in B&B's, forget Gig Harbor. There are no motels. To make B&B reservations or arrange for boat rentals, ☎ 206-851-6865. This is a good jumping-off place to explore south Puget Sound and Vashon Island.

Vashon Island

Vashon, called the Bed & Breakfast Isle, is reachable by ferry from Point Defiance Park in Tacoma or by rental boat in Gig Harbor.

This is a place for people who want to get away from the bustle of daily life. Miles of lightly traveled country roads lace the island's 10-mile length. There are places for beach walking, boat rentals, golf, bird watching and an unusually good Saturday Market. Check out the **Blue Heron Center** for art by local artists.

ACCOMMODATIONS. Overnight visitors may pick from a selection of cottages or bed & breakfast inns, as well as restaurants ranging from gourmet to fast food. Contact the **Vashon Lodging Association** at ☎ 206-463-6763.

Bremerton

Population 38,100

From Tacoma via Highway 16 to Bremerton (via Pearl Harbor) is about 30 miles. A ferry also goes from here to Seattle – a good mini-voyage that operates daily and takes cars and passengers for about $6.50.

I remember this town vividly from 1945. The war was over then and, fresh from the Pacific, I was sent to Bremerton for discharge from the Navy. I couldn't wait for the processing to end, to get on the ferry for Seattle and the train home to Portland. Bremerton, like San Diego, Honolulu or Norfolk, Virginia was awash with the white hats of sailors and unsmiling shore patrol police. Still it was "state side" and there Uncle Sam was doing his level best to get sailors processed and back into civilian life. So I gladly tolerated Bremerton.

Bremerton, with all its history, remains a functioning naval base. It is home to the Pacific Fleet and still has the area's biggest industry – the Puget Sound Naval Shipyard.

During the war, ships of the U.S. Fleet – including five of the battleships bombed at Pearl Harbor – were repaired here. It was here also that many men and women built ships in record time to fight that war.

Visitors to Bremerton should see a pair of historic naval vessels. One of them, the Battleship *Missouri*, proud veteran of WWII and the scene of Japan's surrender on her deck, is near the Seattle Ferry Pier. The other, the Destroyer *Turner Joy* of Vietnam fame, is next to the ferry. Here too is the **Bremerton Naval Museum**, with its display of seagoing history. Entry is by donation.

Beyond Bremerton to the north on Highway 3, about 12 miles, take the Keyport exit to the **Naval Undersea Museum**. Here you will learn about the diversity of the world beneath the sea, particularly in Puget Sound.

ACCOMMODATIONS AND DINING. The Best Western Bay-view Inn, four miles west of the ferry terminal at 5640 Kitsap Way, ☎ 206-373-7349, has good views of the bay, dining room and cocktail lounge. Rates are moderate. Convenient to the ferry at 3400 11th St., ☎ 206-377-0093, the **Dunes Motel** has a restaurant nearby and moderate rates. **Nendel's Suites** at 4303 Kitsap Way, ☎ 206-377-4402, has rates that are moderate and a restaurant nearby.

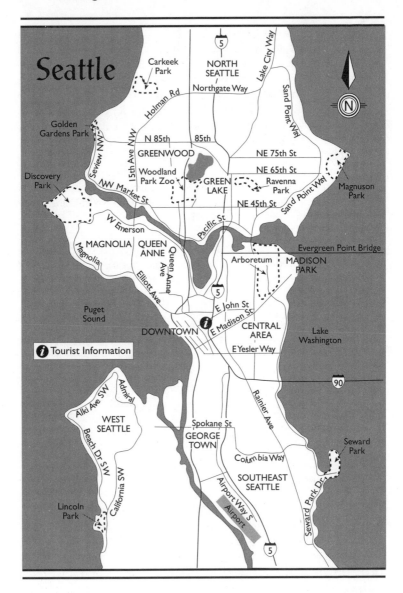

Seattle

Population 616,300 – Metro Area 2,559,200

No discussion of Seattle can begin without mentioning an important point of entry into Washington – Sea-Tac Airport, which is about 20 miles north of Tacoma and 10 miles south of Seattle. It's on Highway 99, just west of I-5. All road maps prominently display this immense facility, a world in itself.

For those who arrive at the airport without hotel reservations, arrangements can be made by calling the **Seattle Hotel** Hotline (between 2:30 am and 5 pm) at ☎ 800-535-7071. This number can be used from anywhere in the U.S.

GETTING INTO TOWN. Rent a car at the airport or, to simply get into town, take the **Gray Line** airport express buses. They leave every 30 minutes and for $5.50 will deliver you to almost any hotel in town. For door-to-door van service, take the **Shuttle Express** for $16-20. To take the **Metro Transit Bus** into Seattle, the cost is about $1.60.

Coming into Seattle by Amtrak train, the station is downtown. From there, Metro Transit buses or taxis will deliver you anywhere.

Seattle, like San Francisco, is nearly surrounded by water. San Francisco, on a peninsula, is hemmed in by the ocean and the bay. Seattle is locked in by Puget Sound and Lake Washington's 18-mile length. But, unlike San Francisco, Seattle is further sandwiched in between mountain ranges – the Olympics to the west and the Cascades, dominated by Mt. Rainier, to the east.

Seattle, named for an Indian known as Sealth, has prospered from its beginning in 1851. Lumber, fur trading, fishing and shipping have contributed to its success. So did the 1897 Klondike Gold Rush, for which the city was the jumping-off point.

When I first saw Seattle in the late 30's, it had the tallest building west of the Mississippi – the 42-story Smith Tower on 2nd and Yesler. Now, reflecting the mountains to the east and west, Seattle has become a high-rise city, an impressive metropolis. The Space Needle is a 605-foot landmark with an observation tower at 520 feet. But, while it's the most visible landmark, the Columbia Tower is taller, with a rotating restaurant and an observation platform at the top.

Coming into Seattle by car along busy I-5, which runs north and south, take an exit for downtown. The Pike Street exit is a good one, as is the Pioneer Square turn off. Then, downtown in the center of things around 5th and Pine, put your car in a parking lot (from $3 an hour to $10 a day) and see downtown on foot or by public bus (free during the day). The "free zone" is between Battery St. to the north, Jackson St. to the south, the waterfront to the west and 6th Ave. to the east. Within this perimeter you'll find the essence of Seattle.

Better yet, consider checking into a hotel and seeing the town at a more leisurely pace.

Hotels

Hotels in this area are abundant and range from pricey to inexpensive. At the upper level there's the old classic, the **Four Seasons Olympic Hotel**. It's a grand Renaissance-style building at 411 University Street. ☎ 206-661-1700. Or consider the **Crowne Plaza**, on 6th and Seneca, ☎ 204-464-1980. **The Mayflower Park Hotel**, at 4th and Olive, ☎ 206-623-8700, is right at the Pike Street Market. **The Seattle Hilton** is at 6th and University, ☎ 206-624-0500. All of the above are expensive. For others in this category, check the handy *AAA Oregon-Washington Tour Book*.

A notch down in price is **The Pacific Plaza** at 400 Spring St., ☎ 800-426-1165, with moderate rates. **The Sixth Avenue Inn**, at 2000 6th Ave., ☎ 800-648-6440, has moderate rates.

For inexpensive accommodation, check the **St. Regis Hotel** at 116 Stewart Street, ☎ 206-448-6366. **The Pacific Hotel**, at 317 Marion Street, ☎ 206-622-3985, is also inexpensive.

Once you're settled in, read the *Seattle Guide*, found in most hotel rooms and, armed with information, set out to see the town.

Touring

See **Pioneer Square**, which is close to the waterfront and is filled with restored buildings reflecting history, including the Klondike Gold Rush. Here too there are sizable numbers of art galleries.

Take a **Seattle Best Walking Tour**. These strolls leave from the Westlake Plaza at 4th and Pine. You are guided on a 2½-hour walk that provides a good picture of Seattle's architecture, art and history. For reservations call ☎ 206-226-7641. The fee is $10.

Don't miss the **Pike Street Market** on 1st St. This unusual market features seafood (often theatrically thrown about by enthusiastic fish dealers), fresh produce, flamboyant street musicians, shops and seafood restaurants by the score. Try not to miss the legendary restaurant, **Ivar's Acres of Clams**, at Pier 54.

The Monorail takes passengers – swiftly – from its terminal at 4th and Pine to the Seattle Center, scene of the 1962 World's Fair and now the site of opera, symphony and other cultural attractions. For a fair of 45¢-90¢, the Monorail will whisk you there in 95 seconds.

In the northwest part of the city, see the **Lake Washington Ship Canal and Locks**. Watch vessels pass though and stop into the Visitor's Center, where docents explain the maritime history of the canal and locks.

Walk to Pier 52 (near Pioneer Square) and take the ferry to **Bainbridge Island**. It runs about once an hour during the day. Bainbridge has the quaint qualities of a fashionable suburb. Wander about the pleasant town of Winslow, perhaps have lunch, or take the "walkabout," a mile-long footpath along the waterfront.

For wine buffs, the **Bainbridge Island Vineyards** are only a quarter-mile north of the ferry landing. It's a fine place to picnic. Then board the ferry and return to Seattle.

The San Juan Islands & The Olympic Peninsula

Going north out of Seattle on I-5, the freeway moves through attractive green urban areas. If you drive it at rush hour, you'll be preoccupied with the traffic. In any case, I advise you head for Anacortes, a good gateway to the San Juan Islands, leaving I-5 at exit 208. From there, continue north on quiet roads that pass verdant farms and fields of cows munching rich grass. Keep going along SR 532 through Stanwood, Milltown, Conway and, eventually, La Conner.

La Conner

Population 700

Pause in this port town, which embodies the flavor of a19th-century fishing port. In La Conner the past has been preserved, buildings have been restored, museums celebrate the mid-1800's, and art galleries display their wares.

Boats to charter, for fishing or sightseeing, can be found at the marina – as can a number of very good seafood restaurants that overlook the harbor. As a suggestion, try the **Lighthouse Inn**. It's excellent.

With Anacortes as a destination, a lunch pause in La Connor, coupled with some wandering, may be enough. But if you want to spend the night, there are plenty of motels ranging from moderate to expensive.

Anacortes

Population 11,500

Sailing off Anacortes.

Here, you're 90 miles north of Seattle in a town that revolves around boating – ferries, power boats and sailing craft.

At the north end of Fidalgo Island, Anacortes is connected by bridge to the mainland and by daily toll ferry serving the San Juan Islands, as well as Sidney on Vancouver Island in Canada. Anacortes is an attractive town, a desirable place to live – and, from nearby Mt. Erie's 1,270 feet, there are fine views of Mt. Rainier, the Olympic Range and the San Juan Islands.

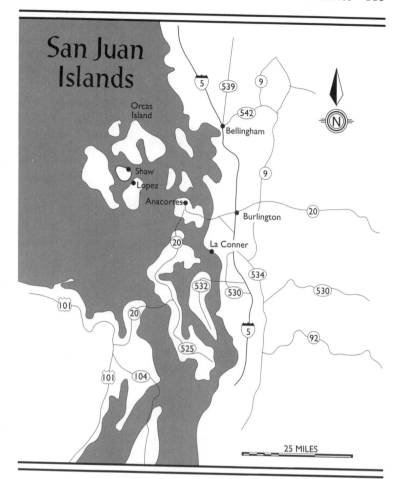

San Juan
Islands

Orcas
Island

Bellingham

Shaw
Lopez

Anacortes

Burlington

La Conner

25 MILES

Where to Stay & Dine

No problem here. There are at least eight top motels and B&B's.
The Anacortes Inn on SR 20, ☎ 800-327-7976, has good views and
a restaurant nearby. Moderate. **The Albatross B&B**, 5708 King's
Way, ☎ 360-293-0677, is in a Cape Cod-style home overlooking a
marina. Moderate. **The Holiday Motel**, with a restaurant, is at 2903
Commercial Avenue, ☎ 360-293-6511. It is inexpensive. **The Ship
Harbor Inn**, a quarter-mile south of the ferry landing, ☎ 800-852-
8586, has fine views and moderate rates. **The Cap Sante Inn**, at 906
9th Street, ☎ 800-852-0846, also has good views and moderate rates.
The Islands Inn, with a restaurant, at 3401 Commercial Avenue, ☎
360-293-4644, has views of Fidalgo Bay and Mt. Baker. Rates are
moderate. Check tourist literature for other motels. When checked
in, wander about town, see the murals on historic buildings, visit

the restored railway station, and take a look at the famous river-boat, *W.T. Preston*.

For good seafood, try **Boomer's Landing** next to Wyman's Marina, ☎ 360-293-5108. Dinners are expensive. French cuisine is served at the **Courtyard Bistro**, downtown on Commercial Street, ☎ 360-299-2923. Moderate. **La Petit**, at Islands Inn Motel, has a varied menu. Moderate. There are plenty of other places to eat in town. Wandering about, they will be obvious.

FERRY BOATS FROM ANACORTES. The Washington State Ferry Service operates ferries from Anacortes to Sidney, B.C. on Vancouver Island. From there, Victoria is easily accessible. En route, they stop at four San Juan Islands: Lopez, Shaw, Orcas, and San Juan, then Sidney. The other 180 islands in the San Juans can be reached only by private or charter boats.

To travel simply, leave your car in Anacortes and board the ferry as a foot passenger or, better yet, with a rental bicycle. Traveling with your car to all four islands, then to Sidney, will cost about $35. Doing it on foot will cost about $7. Be assured that food and accommodations are available on most islands.

Some 17 ferries leave Anacortes every day, but not all of them stop at all the islands. Check schedules at the ferry terminal.

The San Juan Islands

Of the 186 or more islands that make up this group lying within the confines of Puget Sound, only a few are inhabited. Only four are served by ferry. Some are little more than isolated rocks and others are wooded, often with good beaches, fine anchorages and excellent clamming, crabbing and fishing. Camping and hiking are other good possibilities.

Orcas Island

Crowned by 2,400-foot Mt. Constitution, Orcas is the largest of the San Juans. It comprises 57 square miles and has 60 miles of paved road. There are lots of resorts. Some, like **Rosario** with its grand old lodge, are posh. Rates at Rosario, with all possible amenities, range from moderate to luxury. The dining is superb. Others, simpler and less expensive, are favorites with hikers and bikers. There are at least eight places to stay, all listed in the *AAA Tour Book*, that are moderately priced.

Campsites, like **Moran State Park** (with 151 sites ranged around a lake and lots of hiking trails), are popular. But, in high summer, this one may be filled. Call ahead at ☎ 606-376-2326.

Bikes or mopeds can be rented from agencies near the ferry. There are plenty of hills to climb. You will find grocery stores and restaurants to provide sustenance.

San Juan Island

On this island, with its 55 square miles of rolling, wooded hills, dotted with small farms, Friday Harbor is the center of activity. This is where the ferry comes in.

There was a war on this island in 1859. Britain and the U.S were adversaries in a dispute over which country owned the area. Hostilities were mediated by Germany, who decided in favor of the U.S. The casualties amounted to one dead pig.

Recreational possibilities are good here. Kayaking and scuba diving can be arranged from near the ferry landing at **Emerald Sea Aquatics**, ☎ 360-378-2772. For whale watching, visit **Lime Kiln State Park**, 10 miles west of Friday Harbor. From there, in summer, you may see pods of orcas or minke whales.

ACCOMMODATIONS. Friday Harbor boasts several excellent inns, B&Bs and motels. They are all easy to find and are spelled out in the *AAA Oregon-Washington Tour Book*. Expect to pay moderate rates.

Moving about by bike, moped or car, there are several camping sites, as well as several resorts. **San Juan County Park**, about 16 miles from the ferry dock, has good camp sites.

DINING. The Downrigger, in Friday Harbor, has a pleasant lounge with good views. Dinner is moderately priced. For excellent seafood, try **Maloula's** in downtown Friday Harbor. Moderate. **The Spring Tree Café** in downtown Friday Harbor has Euro-bistro-style dining at moderate rates. For informal, less expensive food, try **The Bistro** in town or **The Front Street Café** near the ferry.

Lopez Island

This is a smaller island, hilly and forested, that is marked by isolated coves. Lopez is popular with cyclists who camp at **Odlin County Park, Spencer Spit Park** and at **Agate Beach.**

ACCOMMODATIONS. The Edenwild Inn, in downtown Lopez, ☎ 360-468-3238, has a restaurant nearby and is an elegant choice with moderate rates.

DINING. There are only a few places to eat here. Try the **Bay Café** in Lopez; it has good seafood. **Gails** has everything from hamburgers to sophisticated dining. Inexpensive to moderate.

Shaw Island

Shaw has 10 miles of roads and one campsite at **Indian Cove,** two miles from the ferry. This island is primarily residential and the folks who live there are friendly, but would obviously be happier without the presence of hikers and bikers. There is a store by the ferry landing that can supply camping needs.

Boat Chartering in the San Juans

There are plenty of places to charter boats for sailing or power boating in these islands. In addition to Anacortes, Bellingham is a popular choice, as is Friday Harbor on San Juan Island. Bellingham – 90 miles north of Seattle – has the advantage that it is close to the Northwest route through the San Juans and close to the less-traveled Canadian Gulf Islands. Here are a few charter possibilities.

Penmar Marine Company Yacht Charters, 2011 Skyline Way, Anacortes, WA 98221, ☎ 800-828-7337. **The Anacortes Yacht Charters,** Suite 2, P.O. Box 69, Anacortes, WA, ☎ 800-233-3004. **Charters Northwest,** P.O. Box 915, Friday Harbor, WA, ☎ 800-258-3119. **San Juan Sailing,** 1 Squalicum Harbor Esplanade, Bellingham, WA 98225, ☎ 800-677-7245. These are all knowledgeable organizations, staffed by people who love their work.

If you're a novice and require sailing instruction, **San Juan Sailing** in Bellingham is a good choice. They'll give you a 12-hour basic sailing course with the goal of skippering a 20-39-foot sailboat. They also offer a 32-hour coastal cruising course. Or you can learn coastal navigation and advanced coastal cruising. Cost for the basic sailing course is $149; basic coastal cruising is $175. Query them about other fees, other courses.

Chartering

All chartering companies will want visible proof of your ability to handle the boat of your choice – power or sail. If you're not that experienced, they can provide a skipper for a fee.

What to Bring

Most charters are equipped with everything except food, bedding and towels. Some companies provide rings for crabbing.

Where to Cruise

There are folks who anchor at one of hundreds of bays and coves and never move till it's time to come home. But most people want to go to a different place each day. One itinerary might be a multi-day San Juan cruise, as outlined below.

Sail or power your way out from Anacortes. Turn west under Gueme's Island, which is rich feeding ground for many species of birds. Sail past the three islets that make up Bird Rocks. Watch for seals. Continue on to Cypress Head on Cypress Island and tie up at the buoy. Bottom fishing is good here, as is crabbing.

Next day move on to Sucia Island and moor. Walk the fine trails of Sucia, then spend the night. At this point you're 26 miles from Anacortes.

Sail from Sucia about nine miles to Waldron Island; supplies are available here. Continue south to tiny Jones Island, where there's a herd of deer. Explore the island and spend the night tied up at a buoy.

Next day go south to Friday Harbor on San Juan. If you're there on Saturday night, hitch a ride across the island to Roche Harbor for the "legendary" Saturday night dance. Then, by fits and starts, make your way back to Anacortes via Orcas and Lopez Islands. At the finish, you'll have covered 75-85 beautiful, reasonably calm miles.

Cost

Prices for chartering vary according to the company, the size and type of boat, the season and whether or not you need a skipper. Roughly, though, here is what to expect.

SAILBOATS. For a sailboat, say a 34-foot Catalina, complete with propane stove, roller rigging, shower and BBQ, expect to pay about $1,245 a week in high season, $970 in low season. High season is June through September.

A vessel such as the one above can sleep seven people. If you need a skipper, the charge is about $175/day.

POWERBOATS. They come in all sizes, from 25 feet to 52 feet or more. A middle-sized boat, say a 32-footer that makes 17 knots and sleeps six, could cost about $1,750 per week in high season and $1,350 in low season.

The Olympic Peninsula

Coming from Aberdeen, the Olympic Peninsula is best approached via SR 20 south down Whidbey Island. It's a peaceful trip through wooded farming country, followed by Whidbey's largest town, Oak Harbor (population 17,200). Coupeville comes next, a town with three old block houseS that were built to defend the settlers from Salish Indians. Then comes Keystone, where you take a 40-minute ferry ride to Port Townsend on the Peninsula.

The other route goes north from Olympia. Turn left off I-5 onto 101 and follow it north 100 miles to port Townsend. Along this way, the road passes through Shelton and Hoodsport. This is the Hood Canal approach, running along the inland waterway. You pass many state parks, spectacular marine mountain vistas, and tidal zones rich with clams, oysters and shrimp.

ACCOMMODATIONS ALONG THE WAY. Hoodsport is a good stop. **The Glen-Ayr Canal Resort,** ☎ 360-837-9522, will assist travelers in fishing, clamming and oystering. They will put you up too. Rates are moderate.

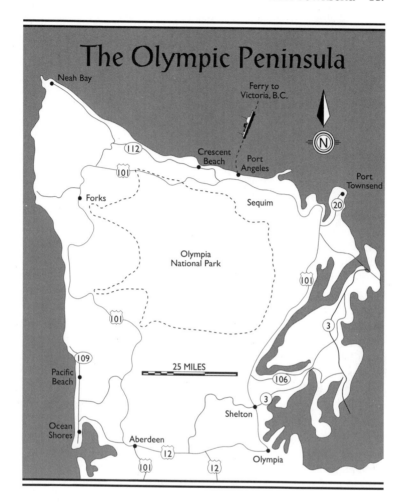

The Olympic Peninsula

Port Townsend

Population 7,000

Port Townsend, at the very top of Puget Sound, has the look of the late 19th century. Its main street runs along the waterfront and boasts a collection of carefully restored wood and brick buildings. There is an ambience about this town that has attracted sizable numbers of artists and craftspeople.

Accommodations

The last time I was there I noticed a hotel, **The Palace**, on Water Street (the main stem). It had the look of the past, with a Victorian style. So I mounted the steps to the reception area (which has an appearance not unlike the entrance to a 19th-century house of ill-repute). The place is elegantly restored. Each room has a title, Miss Lou, Miss Dixie, Miss Annie, which lends more weight to my suspicion that it had a bawdy past.

My room was delightfully well decorated, entirely comfortable, and the next morning a restoring breakfast tray lay at my door. Call them at ☎ 360-385-0773. Rates are moderate.

The Manresa Castle, ☎ 360-358-5750. On the bluff overlooking town, this is another beautifully restored mansion complete with dining room and entertainment. Rates are moderate to expensive. **The James House**, at 1238 Washington Street, ☎ 360-385-1238, is yet another celebration of the past. Moderate to expensive. **The Old Consulate Inn** at 313 Washington Street, ☎ 800-300-6753, is the mansion of Port Townsend's founding family. It serves afternoon tea, a banquet breakfast, evening sherry and has a billiard room. Expensive. There are other, more contemporary accommodations in town, as well.

Dining

There's a ground level restaurant associated with the **Palace Hotel**. It's small, intimate and serves good seafood. The **Café Piccolo**, 3030 Highway 20, offers Italian cooking at moderate prices. The **Landfall**, at 412 Water Street, has inexpensive seafood. The **Silverwater Café**, downtown at 126 Quincy Street, also has good seafood at inexpensive prices. Don't forget **Manresa's** at the Castle, where you drink cocktails in an elegant decor and dine in style for moderate prices.

Port Angeles

Population 17,700

From Port Townsend to Port Angeles is 46 miles. On arrival you're in the largest town on the North Olympic Peninsula. It's the jumping-off place for the Olympic National Park, as well as for Canada-bound travelers. Folks going to Canada can do so aboard ferries of the Black Ball Transport Company, which operates daily service to Victoria, 18 miles away. Or you can take the Victoria Express ferries, which run from mid-May to mid-October. Fares are about $26 one way for car and driver. Foot passengers pay about $24 round-trip.

Port Angeles is, as they say, "where the Olympics meet the sea." Still, the Olympics are some distance from town, as are the other attractions of the Olympic Peninsula. So I suggest only a brief pause in Port Angeles.

DINING. Dine at one of an incredible number of restaurants – then move on. Try **Bushwhackers**, 1527 E. 1st, the **Café Garden** east of town on 101, **Downriggers** at the ferry landing, or the **Golden Gate** Chinese restaurant in town. Have a beer with lunch at **The Wreck**, the oldest tavern in town, at 1025 E. 1st Street.

ACCOMMODATIONS. Places to stay in Port Angeles are plentiful and easily spotted along 101. All are described in the *AAA Oregon-Washington Tour Book*.

NEAR PORT ANGELES. The Olympic National Park and Hurricane Ridge. Leave 101 at Port Angeles, turn south and drive about 19 miles to Hurricane Ridge – which sometimes lives up to its name. From here, at elevation 6,000 feet, views look out at surrounding glacial peaks, Mt.Baker, and across the straits to Vancouver Island.

At Big Meadow, where the lodge is located, there are trails through forested canyons, alpine meadows and views of the highest peak in the Olympic Peninsula – 7,965-foot Mt. Olympus. Ask locally about staying at the lodge.

One important note about the Olympic Peninsula's interior. Several roads enter the interior, but none traverses it. To get deep into the interior, foot or horseback are the only options.

The Elwha River

Consider this river for serene calm one moment and churning white water the next. David King, owner of the **Olympic Raft and Guide Services** (☎ 452-360-1443) says that the Elwha float trip is a good way to see what the Peninsula offers – wildlife, forests and the milky green water of rivers fed by Olympic Mountain glaciers.

To get there go west on 101 about 10 miles to Elwha. But call David King first.

Crescent Lake

From Port Angeles, drive west on 101 past Lake Sutherland, 15 miles. A couple of miles further, Crescent Lake appears. This lake, 8.5 miles long, offers numerous attractions, among them a trail through rainforested grandeur to **Marymere Falls**, a two-mile round-trip walk. Except for a steep stretch on the last quarter-mile, it's an easy trek.

Roads go part way around the north side of the lake, but there is a gap of four or five miles that hikers will enjoy – and it's in this area that a trailhead leads to the top of **Pyramid Peak** – an old WWII lookout.

For moving about on the lake, check out the *Storm King*, a paddle-wheeler that carries passengers on cruises up and down this scenic lake. For reservations, ☎ 206-451-4520.

ACCOMMODATIONS. The **Lake Crescent Lodge** was built in 1937 for President Roosevelt when the national park was first considered. The lodge is on a lovely stretch of the lake, off Highway 101, 21 miles west of Port Angeles. Motel rooms and cottages

Lake Crescent Lodge.

are available. They also offer dining. Rates are moderate. ☎ 206-928-3211. The **Log Cabin Resort** at the east end of the lake, 17 miles west of Port Angeles, offers rooms, cabins, a restaurant, grocery store and recreation. ☎ 206-228-3245. Moderate.

FROM CRESCENT LAKE, continue about 18 miles to Sapho, which has a service station as well as a café. Turn right there (checking the road map), go through Clallam Bay, then continue west to Neah Bay – about 45 miles from Sapho.

Neah Bay

Population tiny

This is a very small village, the most northern community in Washington. It's right on the shores of the Straits of Juan De Fuca, the body of water that leads into Puget Sound, to Victoria, Vancouver, Seattle, Tacoma, and Olympic.

The village is the ancient fishing and cultural center of the Makoh Indian Tribe. Here, in August, they held canoe races, dancing and salmon bakes.

Neah Bay is still excellent for fishing. Charter boats are available. Try **Big Salmon Fishing Resort,** ☎ 206-645-2375, or **Far West Fishing Resort,** ☎ 206-645-2270. Ask them about sleeping accommodations.

To Cape Flattery

This is land's end. At the end of the road from Neah Bay there is a trail, the **Cape Trail,** 7½ miles of often wet footpath that will reward hikers with views of the lighthouse on Tatoosh Island and distant Vancouver Island. Choose a sunny day for this venture.

Forks

Population 3,000

Back on 101 again, from Sapho to Forks is about 18 miles – 56 miles from Port Angeles.

Forks is a popular summer scene for fishing (trout and steelhead) and for rafting trips on the Calawah, Sol Duc, and Hoh Rivers. Check with **Outdoor Ventures** in Forks at ☎ 206-374-6945. A raft trip with them will cost $375, a fishing trip $75-90.

Accommodations & Dining

All of the motels are in full view along 101 and are moderately priced. For dinner, try the **Smokehouse** on 101. It has a pleasant lounge and family-type food. For breakfast, try the small restaurant – popular with the locals – in the center of the town market.

FROM FORKS. On leaving Forks bound south, be sure you're filled up with gas. There are few services between here and Aberdeen, 105 miles away.

The Hoh Rainforest

Drive south from Forks along 101 to the Hoh Rainforest Road, about 14 miles. Turn left and go 19 miles to the campground. It rains more than 100 inches a year here. A jungle of sorts has been the result, not a tropical jungle like Malaysia, New Guinea or Africa, but a temperate one that grows immense ferns, huge trees, Sitka spruce, fir, cedar and maple. This, the lushest rainforest in the U.S. (Hawaii excepted), exists because of the nearby Japanese current and the rain that nurtures moss and verdant underbrush.

HIKING. Take easy one-mile trails, the **Hall of Mosses** and the **Spruce Trail**. For a long trek, do the 17-mile march along the Hoh River to Blue Glacier. If you want more, continue 20 miles further for the assault on Mt. Olympus. Inquire and plan carefully for the latter.

PACIFIC BEACHES. If you drive 10 or 12 miles down 101 from the Hoh Rainforest turnoff, the Pacific comes into view. The road then runs along the coast about 15 miles, past Ruby Beach – its wide strand piled high with driftwood – to Kalaloch.

Kalaloch has a lodge, with cabins on a bluff overlooking the ocean. Clamming on the beach is good and all equipment can be rented. The lodge has a seaview dining room – a fine place to end the day. ☎ 360-962-2271.

Lodge at Kalaloch Beach.

Lake Quinault

Some 30 miles along 101 beyond Kalaloch is the turnoff for Lake Quinault. This lake, at the foot of soaring mountains, surrounded by rainforest, is a place of extreme beauty. It is five miles long and road loops around the lake – some 30 miles of rainforested grandeur.

HIKING. Numerous short trails wander along the lake and into rainforest areas. A six-mile hike leads to the world's largest yellow cedar and the Elwha-Quinault loop covers 45 miles of Olympia National Park.

ACCOMMODATIONS. Lake Quinault Lodge (☎ 360-288-2900) is two miles off 101. It's an historic lodge in a beautiful lakeside setting next to a rainforest. There is a dock with canoes and rental boats and a wide green lawn for lounging. There is dining and entertainment too. Moderate.

Moving south, Aberdeen is about 50 miles futher. Here you join a freeway to Olympia, 50 miles distant.

Lake Quinault Lodge.

Aberdeen

Population 16,600

This town on Gray's Harbor, an important fishing port and lumbering community, is home to handsome Victorian houses that decorate the hills north of downtown.

Aberdeen is also a historic port. Here, there's a replica of Captain Robert Gray's ship, the *Columbia Redidiva*, with which he explored the Northwest Pacific coast in 1792.

ACCOMMODATIONS AND DINING. Good motels abound in this town, most of them on or near 101. The *AAA Oregon-Washington Tour Book* spells out the choices.

Duffy's Restaurant, 1212 East Wishbaw, has a lounge and dining room. Moderate. **Bridges Restaurant** on 112 N. G St. has a lounge and a good, moderately priced dining room.

The North Cascades

The North Cascades National Park is a 505,000-acre preserve in north-central Washington. Roughly speaking, it is the next park north of Rainier National Park and it continues north well into Canada.

North Cascades & Mount Rainier

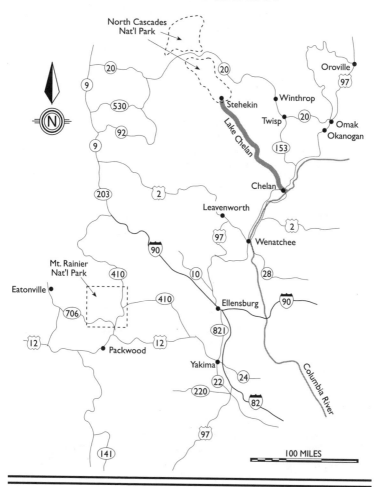

Mt. Baker. At an elevation 10,778 feet, this peak lies within the Mt. Baker National Forest, just west of the North Cascades National Park. To get here from I-5, take SR 542 branching off just north of Bellingham. Drive through Maple Falls, about 38 miles west of Bellingham, and then another 10 miles to Glacier. The road then follows the Nooksack River to the mountain, about 65 miles east of Bellingham.

At Maple Falls there is a bed and breakfast inn, **The Country Hill Bed and Breakfast, ☎** 360-599-1049. At Glacier, there is the **Glacier Creek Motel** and Cabins, **☎** 360-599-2991. The **Mt. Baker Chalet**, **☎** 360-599-2405, is another option. All three are good headquarters for visiting the mountain.

There is a lodge at Mt. Baker open all year. In summer, a chair lift at the lodge takes visitors up to **Panorama Dome**, which has spectacular views.

In winter there are lifts to a selection of runs, where people ski until almost the 4th of July.

To get the **North Cascades National Park**, turn off I-5 at Burlington onto Highway 20 (just north of Mt. Vernon) and continue east, about 190 miles to the town if Twisp. En route you'll have covered the highest passes in the state of Washington – driveable only in high summer. Make this trip with gas tanks fully topped off. There are few services along this remote but spectacular route. About 35 miles east of I-5, there is a turnoff to the north at Concrete. This is the road that leads to **Baker Lakes**, a good spot for fishing, boating and hiking. Other than that one turnoff, you'll be committed to Highway 20.

This drive is a dramatic run, a passage through towering raw rocks, past highland meadows, beside alpine lakes. This is the high country, a magnet for hikers. The forests thin out up here and surrounding peaks, as well as the trail ahead, are sharply defined.

Beyond Concrete, Highway 20 proceeds 100 or so miles through **Rockport**, where there is a State Park with camp sites and hook-ups. There is also **The Totem Trail Motel, ☎** 360-873-4535. You will find good fishing near Rockport in the Sauk River.

Marble Mount comes next, another good wilderness area for camping and hiking. Continue on another 15 miles to the **Goodell**

Creek National Park Campground. Only a short way beyond is Diablo Lake, the gateway to sinuous Ross Lake that winds its way into Canada. Check out the **Ross Lake Resort, ☎** 360-386-4437. This is a popular area for fishermen. Boats can be rented here.

Rainy Pass, at elevation 4,860 feet, appears about 28 miles beyond Diablo. Note that here the Pacific Crest Trail, going down the spine of Washington, Oregon and California, crosses the road. Hikers may want to pause and do stretches of that trail, long or short, or may be happy with an easy path that leads 1½ miles to **Lake Ann**.

Washington Pass, a few miles further on, is still higher and here drivers, even in summer, will probably pass between snow banks that have been pushed aside by the plow.

From there on, you're going downhill, past Mazama to Winthrop.

Winthrop

Population 400
Elevation 1,765

For such a small town, Winthrop has a lot to offer – hiking, biking, boating, dining, golfing, skiing – and it delivers all of this in an "old West" style. With its wooden sidewalks, vintage street lights and frontier-style wooden buildings, Winthrop belongs in the late 19th century. Owen Wister, author of *The Virginian*, lived here early this century and he commented on the town and its inhabitants in his novel. For more of the past, step into the **Shafer Museum** downtown and examine the pioneer structures – a print shop, a general store, a log cabin, an early doctor's office and an outdoor collection of turn-of-the-century mining equipment.

ACCOMMODATIONS. All of the following have moderate rates. **Hotel** Rio Vista is right downtown on the Metow River, ☎ 509-996-3535. The **Marigot Hotel** is on SR 20, ☎ 509-996-3100. **Sun Mountain Lodge** is a resort, with dining room, 10 miles west of' town off SR 20, ☎ 509-996-2211. It offers such activities as horseback riding, fishing, and river rafting. **The Virginian Resort**, on the Metow River at the south end of town, is on SR 20, ☎ 509-996-2535. **The Winthrop Inn** is one mile east on SR 20, ☎ 509-996-2217. **Winthrop Mountain View Chalets** is at the south end of town, ☎ 509-996-3113.

DINING. The Duck Brand Restaurant, 248 Riverside, has a homey atmosphere and offers good Yankee food. Beer and wine are served. Dinners are moderately priced. Sun Mountain Lodge Dining Room, in the lodge of the same name, has a scenic view, good, hearty food, and includes a cocktail lounge. Dinners are expensive. The Virginian Restaurant, at the resort, has a cocktail lounge and serves food with a local flavor in a cedar log dining room. Dinners are moderately priced.

Twisp

Population 900
Elevation 1590

This is a pretty little town, 11 miles beyond Winthrop at the scenic confluence of the Twisp and Methow Rivers. What grows here is of importance to the community – lumber, apples and farming. But Twisp does have a reputation among river runners. Osprey River Adventures, ☎ 509-997-4416, offers a spirited whitewater trip for $60 (including wet suit). There is also a scenic trip for $50.

ACCOMMODATIONS AND DINING. The Idle-a-While Motel, ☎ 509-997-3222, on SR 20, has a restaurant. It is inexpensive.

Beyond Twisp, to the east, western Washington lies waiting.

Stehekin

This is a perfect place for trekkers and campers, made even more so by the fact that you can only reach it by boat or plane. Or you can backpack in on the Pacific Crest Trail, coming south from Rainy Pass on Highway 20. Check this latter approach carefully before setting out.

GETTING THERE. Scheduled transportation by boat from Chelan is available year round. The Lake Chelan Boat Company, ☎ 509-682-2224, has two boats that make the trip. Scenery along the way is spectacular. Fares are $21-$38 round-trip. Some visitors head up and back the same day, though each way takes several hours.

ACCOMMODATIONS AND DINING. The Stehekin Lodge, open year round, offers lodging, dining and boating. Campers can buy groceries here as well. Rates are moderate. Because there's only one public phone in the area, I'd suggest a call to the Lake Chelan Chamber of Commerce for information on reservations and costs. ☎ 800-424-3526.

Camping at Stehekin is free. But a locally obtained permit is required.

HIKING. There are many trails into the North Cascades from Stehekin and there are easy loop hikes. Check out the **Purple Creek Trail** and the **Company Creek Trail**. Ask about these and others at the Stehekin Visitors Center.

Mount Rainier National Park

Mount Rainier is visible from many parts of Washington and, at 14,410 feet, is an imposing giant. In his book, *Backgrounds of Washington*, Archie Satterfield calls Mt. Rainier nature's Ninth Symphony of Beethoven.

Compared to climbing other Cascade mountains, where you put one foot ahead of the other and eventually succeed, Mt. Rainier is a challenge. I've got friends, experienced climbers, who have failed in the attempt. This climb takes planning, perseverance and plain good luck.

TO GET THERE. Check out road maps carefully and note that there are several routes. One of the best involves a loop run, a trip completely around Rainier to the east, then back via SR 418 to I-5 near Tacoma.

Begin by leaving I-5 south of Chehalis and drive along SR 508 to Morton. Continue on from Morton about 20 miles to SR 706, which you take to **Longmire**, the park headquarters. There is also a visitors center here. For hikers, good trails radiate from here. Beyond Longmire, the road twists and turns its way up, till at Paradise, after about 14 miles, you're at 5,400 feet.

Paradise is a major staging point for the climb up Rainier. It's also the beginning of one of America's finest walks, **the Wonderland Trail**, a 92-mile footpath that encircles the entire mountain. It is only open from mid-July to mid-September.

For hiking-camping on the more than 300 miles of trails in Rainier Park, a permit is required – available, along with trail maps, at park headquarters. One thing permitted without license is trout fishing which, with any luck, may augment your camp meals.

The first section of the Wonderland Trail is a 30-mile stretch running from Paradise to **Sunrise** that exposes hikers to lakes, glaciers, falls and a curious canyon. From Sunrise to **Carbon River** is 16½ miles. Along this leg you'll see **Winthrop Glacier**, which originates in the summit ice cap, then **Mystic Lake**. **Carbon Glacier** comes next, a glacier born of snows in a valley head.

From Carbon River to **Longmire** is a 39-mile trek, where you'll see many lakes and much profound beauty. The final section, from Longmire to Paradise, is only six miles and is good for viewing waterfalls.

TO CLIMB THE MOUNTAIN. Check with the Park Superintendent for current regulations, the required permit, climbing instruction and guides. Then set out on what is usually a three-day operation. One day of the three will be for instruction; the next two will be devoted to the climb, which starts from Paradise.

Some routes to the summit are only for experienced mountaineers, while others are somewhat gentler. With a guide, proper equipment and plenty of fortitude, you stand a good chance.

FURTHER HIKING. Pick up the book, *50 Hikes in the Mt. Rainier National Park*, at a park visitors center. This book will go into detail, far better than I can do. It will lead you along the three-mile Carbon River Trail; on a two-mile trek among immense first growth trees along the Ohanapecosh River; on a hard five-mile walk up Skyline Trail to 6,800-foot Panorama Point. Those are three of the 50 hikes described.

ACCOMMODATIONS. For hikers, there are primitive campgrounds, with potable water and simple toilets. These occur along the trail about eight miles apart.

There are more civilized campsites for autos and RV's that provide water and toilets at places like Sunshine Point on SR 706 near the Nisqually Entrance. White Rock is another, a high beautiful place off SR 410, on White River Road. There's also Cougar Rock, off SR 706. This one is near the final portion of the Wonderland Trail.

Charges for staying at these campgrounds are about $5-$8 per site.

There are two comfortable and attractive inns, close to trails and with good views. **The National Park Inn**, in Longmire, ☎ 206-569-2275, has moderate rates and a good dining room. **The Paradise Inn**, ☎ 206-569-2275, also is moderately priced, with a dining room.

For further information, write **The Superintendent, Mount Rainier National Park**, Tahoma Woods, Star Route, Ashford, WA 89304. Or ☎ 206-569-2211.

Eastern Washington & the Upper Columbia River

One very direct way east, say from Seattle, is to get on Route I-90 and take the freeway to Ellensburg, 111 miles. Then continue straight to Spokane, another 174 miles, and only some 20 miles from Idaho. You'll have crossed a great state that way, but you'll miss a lot in the process.

Instead, I'll suggest you might begin your tour eastward from a town in Central Washington we've already looked at – Twisp – at the end of the North Cascade run along SR 20. From there, head on to the town of Chelan.

Chelan

Population 3,000

From Twisp, traveling along the Methow River, then to Columbia, Chelan is about 55 miles. There you've arrived at the southeast end of 55-mile-long **Lake Chelan**. This beautiful lake, narrow and surrounded by mountains, is more than 1,500 feet deep.

The town of Chelan is a resort community filled with possibilities for fun – sailing, water skiing, beaches, hiking, eating and living it up in the resorts and motels. But the best reason to come here is to catch the ferry to Stehekin, 55 miles away at the other end of the skinny lake.

Eastern Washington &
The Upper Columbia River

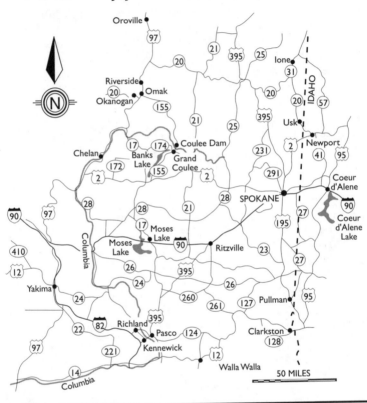

ACCOMMODATIONS AND DINING. Campbell's Resort, 104 Woodin Ave., ☎ 800-553-8225, with dining room, is moderately expensive. **The Apple Inn**, 1002 Woodin Avenue, ☎ 509-682-4044, has moderate rates.

Goochis Restaurant, 104 E. Woodin Ave., has a cocktail lounge and serves good food at moderate rates. Places in town for burgers and fast food exist as well.

Okanogan

Population 2,300

Coming north from Chelan, along both the Columbia River and the Okanogan River, Highway 97 enters Okanogan after 60 miles. The area is known as "Okanogan Country." To some, this means the rolling treeless hills of cowboy country, dude ranches and all. To others, it means old and historic ghost towns or it means fishing, boating and camping. There are three campgrounds near Okanogan – **Leader Lake**, with 16 campsites; **Rock Creek**, with six; and **Rock Lakes**, with eight. There are plenty of hiking trails as well. For information about these camps, call the **Okanogan Visitor Information Service** at ☎ 509-422-1541.

For history buffs, a visit to the **Okanogan County Historical Museum** on Second Ave. will bring the past alive, especially the photos taken by Frank Matsura, a Japanese who settled here in 1903. Entrance is by donation.

ACCOMMODATIONS. The Okanogan Motor Lodge on Second Ave., ☎ 509-422-0400, is inexpensive.

Omak

Population 4,100

Omak, six miles north of Okanogan on Highway 97, is a center for apple growing and lumbering. It is also home to the spirited Omak Stempede, held in August.

This town is a pleasant place, made even more so by the presence of 110 acres of parks, a golf course, and a campsite with full hook-ups for RV's and spaces for tents.

ACCOMMODATIONS. There's a scattering of easily found motels in town – six or seven of them, with rates from inexpensive to moderate. For further information, call the **Omak Chamber of Commerce** at ☎ 800-225-6625.

Riverside

Only six to eight miles north of Omak, Riverside sits on the grassy banks of the Okanogan River. Long ago this was a riverboat stop for steamers that served the valley.

Now this is farm country and apples are grown here. There are four nearby resorts that offer camping, boat rentals and fishing. Bonaparte Lake has good spring fishing. And one of the largest outlets for western clothing in the northwest is located here.

Oroville

Population 1,500

This little town, close to excellent camping at Lake Osoyoos, is a place to restore yourself with good swimming. There is camping and fishing as well. For camping information, ☎ 509-476-3321.

Oroville also has a new micro-brewery that welcomes guests. Contact **Buchanan Brewing Company** at ☎ 800-559-2889.

ACCOMMODATIONS. The Red Apple Inn, on Main Street, ☎ 509-476-3794, is inexpensive. There are restaurants nearby.

Grand Coulee & the Dam

To reach this area, go back down Highway 97 to Omak. Then cross the Colville Indian Reservation along SR 155 through Nespelem to Grand Coulee – about 60 miles.

The work "Coulee" means "large canyon." There were many coulees here before the immense dam was built in the 30's during the Depression.

I remember the days of its construction when friends of my parents happily left home to work on the behemoth that eventually transformed the land's raw beauty to productive green and provided the northwest with enough electricity to support new industry.

With the completion of the dam around 1941, huge Banks Lake and Franklin D. Roosevelt Lake were formed. Now they are popular for boating, camping and good trout fishing. Houseboats can be rented at Lake Roosevelt, ☎ 800-268-5332.

As to the dam itself, its huge concrete mass, one of the biggest in the world, functions in flood control, produces electric power and makes Columbia River water available for irrigation. The complete story of the dam is spelled out at the Visitors Arrival Center. Self-guided tours of the dam are available – and so is a dramatic laser light show projected onto the face of the dam.

ACCOMMODATIONS AND DINING. Travel from Grand Coulee south down the east side of 28-mile-long Banks Lake to **Coulee City**. Several resorts here offer good water sports.

Keep going south through arid land, to **Soap Lake**. This body of water is thought to have therapeutic effects – note the soapy, frothy quality of its water. There are hot springs here as well.

From Soap Lake, continue along SR 17 another 18 miles to Highway 282, then 14 more miles to Moses Lake.

Moses Lake

Population 11,200

Here, 75 miles south of Grand Coulee, is the turn off to busy I-90 bound for Spokane. This is a popular stop for folks coming from, or going to, Seattle and Spokane.

There are many lakes around town, but Moses Lake west of town is a favorite of locals because of its warm waters.

ACCOMMODATIONS AND DINING. There are several moderately priced accommodations at lakeside and there are motels nearby in town. Try the **Holiday Inn** at exit 179 off I-90, ☎ 509-766-2000. Rates are moderate and restaurants are nearby.

Ritzville

Population 1,700

From Moses Lake to Spokane is 105 miles. It's a straight run through wide open rolling country, with views that stretch for miles. Ritzville, an oasis-like place I've always enjoyed, usually for lunch, appears about 50 miles east of Moses Lake.

It's got a congenial downtown area with a pair of museums. There is a golf course as well, but it's mainly a town where the gas stations are busy and the restaurants filled with travelers.

Ritzville had the honor of being seriously dumped on by ash from the Mt. St. Helens eruption in May of 1980.

ACCOMMODATIONS AND DINING. I like to stay at a small, friendly motel downtown, the **Colwell Motor Inn,** ☎ 509-659-1620. I've equally enjoyed dining at a small restaurant nearby that is filled with happy locals.

Spokane

Population 177,200

From Ritzville to Spokane is an easy 60 miles. There are few impediments to traffic along this stretch of wide open, gently rolling country, that becomes spotted with pine woods as you approach Spokane. This is the biggest city in eastern Washington, the second in the state. It is where Bing Crosby was raised, where he went to Gonzaga University and it's also the site of the World's Fair Expo 74, the one that left the city with a smart Riverfront Park and a handsome Civic Center.

Note that, before entering Spokane on I-90, the International Airport is just off the freeway to the north. Then, if you're not careful, it's easy to drive right through Spokane and find yourself leaving town. Don't let that happen.

To get the essence of Spokane – to stay, wander, play and eat – leave I-90 on Lincoln Street, Wall Street or Washington Street. Proceed north only a few blocks to Spokane's Skywalk area, where there's a system of covered walkways that connect more than 15 blocks of downtown shops, restaurants and hotels. Just steps away from there, connected by footpaths and vintage trolleys, is Riverfront Park.

Accommodations

The **Davenport Hotel** on Post and Sprague is due to reopen for business in 1996. This historic hotel has long been considered the "grand dame" of hotels on the west coast. It had old world charm – including a wonderful mezzanine with desks and comfortable chairs where commercial travelers could quietly write up their orders and justify expense accounts. The Davenport boasted world-class dining rooms, a fashionable roof top lounge as well as shops. It was a well-loved, gracious Spokane landmark. Perhaps it will be again.

Cavanaugh's Inn at the Park, 303 N. River Road, ☎ 509-326-8000, with two restaurants, lounges and free parking, is right in Riverfront Park. Expensive. **Cavanaugh's River Inn**, on N. River Road, ☎ 509-326-5577, has a restaurant, a lounge, pool and free parking. Moderate. The **Spokane Riverside Plaza** at Riverfront Park, ☎ 800-848-960, has every amenity. Expensive. **West Coast Ridpath Hotel**, 515 W. Sprague, ☎ 800-426-0270, right downtown, has free parking, two restaurants, and moderate prices. **The Towne Center Motor Inn**, 101 W. 1st Ave. ☎ 800-247-1041, is moderate. **The Suntree Inn**, 211 S. Division, ☎ 800-888-6630, is several blocks from the center of town, a cheerful place and inexpensive.

At a distance from downtown to the east, the **Maple Tree Inn**, ☎ 509-535-5810, 4824 E. Sprague St., is inexpensive. **The Spokane Valley Super 8**, 2020 N. Argonne, ☎ 800-800-8000, has moderate rates.

The Spokane Visitor's Guidebook lists other motels, of which there are many.

Dining

Ankeny's 'top of the Ridpath serves fashionable American cuisine with a view; expensive. **Luigi's Italian Restaurant**, downtown at 113 N. Bernard, voted "Best Restaurant of the Year," is moderate. **China Best**, 223 W. Riverside, serves Chinese food. Moderate. **O'Doherty's Irish Grille**, across from the carousel in Riverfront Park, serves steaks and burgers, washed down with good ale, beer and Guiness; inexpensive. **Riverside Thai Restaurant**, in Riverfront Park, is moderate. **Niko's II**, 725 Riverside, serves authentic Greek food and has moderate prices. **The Onion Restaurant**, downtown on Riverside and Bernard, has barbecued ribs, burgers, fine salads, cocktails too; inexpensive. **Finnerty's Red Lion Inn**, on Main and Division, a sports club complete with big screen, has casual dining and moderate prices.

What to See

Riverfront Park is a green, broad patch of land laced with trees, running water, falls and walking paths. It's a 100-acre piece of landscaping born out of the 1974 Expo on two branches of the Spokane River.

Going through this park is a portion of the 37-mile **Centennial Trail**, a track that starts at the Washington-Idaho border, continues through the park, and well beyond, to Milepost 37.

Strolling in the park, you will encounter the **Gondola Skyride**, which carries folks over the falls of the Spokane River. A short way beyond is the **IMAX Theatre**, where a 70 MM movie is projected on a five-story screen. For information, ☎ 509-625-6612.

In the park there are stands for hamburgers, hot dogs, places to ride rollercoasters, to catch the brass ring from a well-preserved carousel and to see a 1902 clocktower that commemorates Spokane's pioneer past.

Also worthy of note are the **Opera House**, the **Convention Center**, and the 1895 **County Court House** that looks like a French château. Then too, all within walking range, is the **Schade Brewery**, with its outlet for antiques, and a **Farmers Market**.

To the south, only steps away, is the **Skywalk**, whose covered walkways deliver shoppers to Bon Marché, Nordstrom's, and other stores, as well as to banks, drug stores and restaurants.

You can walk from downtown on the Centennial Trail to **Gonzaga University**, 502 E. Boone Ave. Bing Crosby was an alumnus. Memorabilia from his life are shown – pipes, records, photos and trophies.

Don't neglect attractions outside the downtown area. **Manito Park**, south of town on Grand Ave., has a Rose Garden, Lilac Garden and a Japanese Garden. For golfers there are 19 public courses in and around the city – to say nothing of winter skiing and the delights of Idaho's close-by Lake Coeur d'Alene.

Pend Oreille County

This unusually good hiking, fishing, camping country in the north-eastern corner of the state – bordered by both Canada and Idaho – was named "Pendant d'Oreille" (ear pendant). That may have originated with Indians, who wore shells hanging from their ears. Since then, not much has happened to mar the beauty of this area, which saw a gold rush in the mid-19th century and later successes with logging, farming and cattle.

But now recreation is an important draw. There are 55 lakes, miles of primitive forest, rivers filled with trout and mountains that are home to caribou, mountain goats, big horn sheep, bear, osprey and geese. All of this within a county 22 miles wide and 67 miles long.

GETTING THERE FROM SPOKANE. Go north from Spokane on Highway 395, then branch off on SR 2 to Newport, right on the Idaho line. Newport is about 45 miles north of Spokane. This is the place to begin exploring the country on either side of the Pend Oreille River – a good 55 miles of it.

Newport

Population 1,780

This town (the Washington-Idaho line goes right through it) is an attractive way point for travel on to Sand Point and Lake Pend Oreille in Idaho. But to do the Pend Oreille River and associated lakes – for hiking, camping, fishing and searching out the past – it's best to pause here, then make your way down the river (north) about 55 miles to Metaline.

ACCOMMODATIONS AND DINING. The Golden Spur, on SR 2, ☎ 208-447-3823, has an adjacent restaurant and lounge; moderate. **Newport City Center Inn**, on SR 2 downtown, is also moderately priced.

For food, try the **Golden China**, on SR 2 west of town. For casual dining, step into **Kelly's Tavern** downtown. This is in Newport's oldest building, a place with a bar that was shipped around Cape Horn on a sailing vessel. Get pizza at the **Pizza Parlor** downtown. Try **Faye's Steakhouse** at the bridge in Old Town. The **Pend Oreille Restaurant & Lounge** downtown is a happy place.

Usk

Unincorporated

Usk is about 18 miles north of Newport on SR 20. It's a good jumping-off point – by marginal road – for such places as **Browns Lake Campground**, where there are 18 sites and a boat launch (no motor boats allowed). Trout fishing in the lake is good, but it must be fly fishing. For hiking, do the 6.4-mile walk to **Bead Lake**. The trailhead is off Forest Service Road 3215, east of Usk.

ACCOMMODATIONS AND DINING. The Inn at Usk, a B&B, ☎ 509-445-1526, is moderately priced. For campers there's **Keo's Korner**. It offers gas, boat launching and food. ☎ 509- 445-1294.

Cross over the river at Usk and you're in **The Kalispel Indian Reservation**. Buffaloes are raised by tribe members and can be seen; ☎ 909-445-1147.

Ione

Population 575

This tiny town has gas, groceries, restaurants, lodging and a city park with a boat landing on the river. More importantly, it's from here that a train runs north to Mataline, about 12 miles. The two-hour round-trip goes along the Pend Oreille River and crosses high over Box Canyon, then goes through a long tunnel. It's an excellent ride. Fare is $4. ☎ 509-442-3397.

Big Meadow Lake, west of Ione, has campsites, good fishing, an interpretive trail and a tower for wildlife viewing.

ACCOMMODATIONS. The Pend Oreille Inn, ☎ 509-442-3418, is moderately priced. **The Plaza Motel**, ☎ 509-442-3418, is also moderate. **The Ione Motel** and RV Park, ☎ 509-442-3213, is inexpensive.

Mataline & Mataline Falls

These two tiny towns (population 200 and 305, respectively) lie on either side of the river. Both provide gas, food and lodging. Better yet, they are close to the back country wilderness areas.

Start close in by visiting **Boundary Dam**, north of town, where mountain goats can be seen on nearby Mt. Linton. Go east of town, to the south end of **Sullivan Lake**, where there is a feeding area for big horn sheep. Good camping sites can be found here too.

HIKING. The Flame Creek Trail 502 is off Forest Service Road 350, south of Mataline Falls. There are some campsites along this four-mile walk, but little water. For the **Salmo Basin Trail 506**, the trail head is off Road #2220, N.E. of Mataline Falls in the Gypsy Peak area. This is an 8.8-mile hiking or horse packing trail, with lots of wildlife, good camping and plenty of water. **Pan Creek-Grassy Top Trail** has its trail head off Road 22 at Pan Creek. This is a scenic, moderately difficult trail with little water. It's in grizzly bear country. For a difficult trek, try the **Kalispel-North Baldy Trail 103**, a seven-mile hike. Check with the Pend Oreille County Trails for this one. ☎ 208-443-2512.

Another moderately difficult trail into caribou and grizzly bear country is the 7.5-mile pack or walking **Jackson Mountain Trail**. Check the above phone number. Go well prepared; these are isolated regions.

FISHING. North of Mataline at **Boundary**, just shy of the Canadian border, is a "walk in" place for rainbow trout fishing. **Huff**, at 3,185 feet elevation, is near the **Stagger Inn Campground**, east of Mataline Falls. You walk in two miles. Good fishing.

In this area there are literally dozens of lakes and river sites for fishing and good hiking. These are areas (true everywhere) where you pack out what you bring in and treat the land with care.

While on the scene in this beautiful region, pick up a copy of *The Pend Oreille County Travel Guide*. It covers this country admirably.

ACCOMMODATIONS IN MATALINE. Try the **Washington Hotel**, a delightful historic inn that was built in 1910. It contains the original furniture and there's a café there too; ☎ 509-446-4415. Moderate.

From Pend Oreille County, I suggest the long junket south to Walla Walla, roughly 250 miles. But don't go straight through. Plan to make some pauses en route, one of which should be Coeur d'Alene, Idaho, and its lake.

To do this, cross the river at Newport (Pend Oreille County) into Idaho and go south on SR 41 to Coeur d'Alene – about 45 miles.

Coeur D'Alene, ID

Population 26,611

Coeur d'Alene, 32 miles east of Spokane, on I-90, is the county seat of Kootenai County and the sixth largest city in Idaho.

Where it sits on the sparkling lake that serpentines its way 23 miles south makes it not only a good place to live but a playground for boaters, hikers, skiers, shoppers, golfers and for thousands of convention delegates.

Downtown Coeur d'Alene has everything visitors want, from trendy boutiques, to book stores, to coffee houses where jazz groups play while you sip. There are fashionable deli's, restaurants of every persuasion and art galleries where western and native American art is sold. Car lovers too will find redemption at the "Auto Classics" on Lakeside Avenue, where Porsches, Mercedes, Ferraris and Corvettes are shown and sold.

GOLF. Play the crown jewel of Northwest golf at the **Coeur d'Alene Resort Golf Course**. This has been selected by *Golf Digest* as America's most beautiful golf resort, a facility famous for the world's only floating green. It's open to the public.

There are other less expensive courses too, such as the **Coeur d'Alene Public Golf Course** and **Avondale-on-Hayden Public Course**.

LAKE CRUISES. Cruises on the lake are done for brunch, dinner, for fishing or for sightseeing. Prices vary. ☎ 208-661-0276.

BOAT RENTALS. Sailing is popular, with lots of exotic places to go. There are houseboats too, and ski boats, canoes and paddle boats. ☎ 208-664-6687.

HIKING. Do the self-guided **Tubbs Hill Walk**, a three-mile nature hike around the peninsula near the lakeside resort. Check out the **Centennial Trail** that runs along the lake. Stroll the **Boardwalk**, the longest floating boardwalk in the world, near the resort. There are plenty of hiking trails in the surrounding mountains.

PARASAILING. Take off from the back of a boat and soar like a bird over the lake. ☎ 208-765-5367.

The list of activities goes on and on – from romantic marriages, seeing locally produced shows, riding double-decker London buses, biking, and horseback riding, to river rafting, swimming, tennis, or visiting antique shops. There's something for everyone here.

Accommodations

The most prestigious place to stay is in the **Coeur d'Alene Resort**. This tower hotel has every conceivable amenity – indoor swimming pool, exercise studios, jacuzzis, sauna, steam room, indoor golf, bowling, racquetball, etc., etc. On the seventh floor is the hotel's signature restaurant, Beverly's. They offer specialty cocktails, hors d'oeuvres and wonderfully served dinner fare, all overlooking the lake. Then, at dockside, the lobby-level restaurant serves fine brunches, dinner and lunches too.

There's a ballroom at the resort and a major conference center – something for everyone, from sophisticated nightlife to activities for the kids.

Golfers should consider the Golf Package rates at the resort. These include accommodations, along with water taxi service to the course, plus a cart for each twosome. Prices, based on double occupancy, range from $99 to $239. For reservations, ☎ 800-688-5253.

Other accommodations are easily found all over town. I come up with at least 40 motels and resorts, some 20 B&B's and 23 campgrounds in or near town.

Dining

Restaurants abound here, from fast food to gourmet, from inexpensive to pricey. Dine at the **Dockside** or in **Beverly's** at the resort. Have a lakefront dinner at the **Beachhouse**, just east of town on Lake Drive. It is moderate to expensive. Enjoy good Italian meals at **Tito Macaroni's**, 210 Sherman, downtown. Moderate. Eat while listening to live jazz and blues at **Jimmy D's Wine Cellar**, downtown at 313 Sherman. Moderate. For Japanese food, try **The Takara** at 309 Lakeside Ave. Moderate. Barbecued ribs, along with a kids' menu is provided at **Rustler's Roost**, at 819 Sherman. Moderate. Dine at **The Cedars Floating Restaurant**, on the Spokane River, near the resort. Moderate to expensive. Have breakfast at the **International House of Pancakes**, on I-90 and 4th St. For Mexican food, there is the **3rd St. Cantina**, 201 N. 3rd. Inexpensive. Wander about town; you'll find lots more.

For further information and a copy of the *Guide to Coeur D'Alene*, call the Visitors Bureau at ☎ 208-664-0587.

From Coeur d'Alene

Continue south (still in Idaho) about 70 miles to Potlatch, Idaho. Turn west on SR 30 and go 10 miles to Palouse, Washington. This town, with its collection of well-cared-for old buildings, is in an area of rolling hills and sculpted fields of wheat. The landscape, with the changing colors of its hills and the sharp shadows they throw, is as restful to the eye as it is productive.

NEAR PALOUSE. For a view of the countryside, go to **Kamiak Butte**. Climb to the summit of the 3,400-foot butte. Have a picnic in the wooded area at the top and capture the ever-changing, shadowed country below on film.

Steptoe Butte, north of town off Highway 195, has local history born of an old settler from England who built a (now gone) hotel on the butte. He died there.

In Palouse you're in the shadow of Washington State University (25 minutes to the south).

Pullman

Population 23,500

This is home to Washington State University and to their dauntless football team, the Cougars. Ten miles away, across the border in Idaho, is a similar community, Moscow, home to the University of Idaho. Academic and social activities of both schools intermix.

Pullman, a comfortable town, has well-maintained, tree-shaded residential areas and a pronounced academic environment, where the humanities are taught along with veterinary medicine, engineering and agriculture. You can add to all this the student-inspired nightlife activities. Pullman is also an ideal hub for further exploration of this lovely country.

While in town wander the handsome W.S.U. Campus. Spend time at the **Art Museum** and the **Anthropology Museum**, both on campus. Follow these intellectual efforts with some after-dark wandering in town, where you can eat well, enjoy yourself, then settle in to one of many motels.

ACCOMMODATIONS AND DINING. American Travel Inn, 515 S. Grand, ☎ 509-334-3500. Inexpensive. **Cougar Land Motel**, 120 Main, ☎ 509-334-3535. Inexpensive. **Holiday Inn Express**, 1190 Bishop Road, ☎ 509-344-4437. Moderate.

There are lots of places to eat and play. For both, try **Peters Bar and Grill**, 1100 Johnson. Inexpensive. **Swilly's Café and Gathering Place**, downtown, is inexpensive. **Mandarin Wok Restaurant**, 115 Grand Ave., has quality Chinese food at moderate prices.

There are plenty of other places for pizza, burgers, Mexican, all of them easy to spot.

FROM PULLMAN. To Walla Walla, via Clarkston and Lewiston, Idaho, is about 127 miles.

Clarkston

Population 6,800

This town and its Idaho neighbor, the larger Lewiston – both named after the intrepid explorers, Lewis and Clark – are set on the Snake River among barren hills. For folks on cruise vessels from Portland, this is the end of the line. From here, passengers going on up Hells Canyon board small metal-hulled boats for a thrilling 50-mile trip through one of the deepest gorges in north America. This is a trip with plenty of wild white water, cliffs bearing Indian petroglyphs, and riverside stretches where big horn sheep, mule deer and wild turkeys frolic.

Some do the round-trip in one day. Others spend the night in a lodge at the far end. Prices vary, but for current information call **Alaska Sightseeing, Cruise West** in Seattle, ☎ 800-426-7702.

ACCOMMODATIONS AND DINING. Quality Inn, 700 Port Dr., ☎ 509-758-9500. Moderate. **Best Western River Tree Inn**, 1257 Bridge St., ☎ 509-758-9557, is moderate to expensive. **Astor Motel**, 1201 Bridge St., ☎ 509-758-9345, is moderate.

Campers can try the **Golden Acres RV Park**, ☎ 509-758-9345. Added to these are the many motels in neighboring Lewiston. Restaurants abound. Try the dining room at the **Quality Inn** in Clarkston, or drive the main stem in Lewiston and choose one of the lively after-dark watering spots.

FROM CLARKSTON. Going west along Highway 12 through rolling, often bare hills, Walla Walla is 97 miles.

Walla Walla

Population 26,500

This pleasant town, site of a private school known for academic excellence – Whitman College – is a comfortable place to live, visit and work. However, the locals are not filled with mirth when outsiders make remarks about the town being so nice it was named twice, or "other than Whitman College and Walla Walla onions, what goes on here?"

Not many tourists visit this attractive town. I like to stop here for that reason.

WHAT TO SEE. West of town, see the **Whitman Museum**. This is where a massacre occurred in 1847, when Marcus Whitman, a missionary, his wife and 11 others were killed by some of his "converted" Cayuse Indians. The Mission has been restored as it was then. For information, ☎ 509-522-6360.

Fort Walla Walla is southwest of town. There's a reconstructed fort, a pioneer village and a cemetery, with the graves of U.S. soldiers and Nez Perce warriors from the 1877 battle so valiantly waged by Chief Joseph.

ACCOMMODATIONS AND DINING. Walla Walla Travelodge, 421 E. Main St, ☎ 503-529-4940. Moderate. **Tapadero Inn**, on 2nd Ave. downtown, ☎ 800-772-8277, is inexpensive. **City Center Motel**, 627 W. Main, ☎ 509-529-2660, is also inexpensive. **Pony Soldier Motor Inn**, 325 E. Main, ☎ 509-529-4360, is moderate to expensive.

A place pleasantly filled with locals is an Italian restaurant downtown – **Pastime Café, ☎** 509-525-0873. This is an old Walla Walla source of wholesome, filling Italian food, washed down with hearty wine. Inexpensive.

Consider the **Merchant's Hotel** on Main St. Inexpensive. Look around and explore other possibilities.

FROM WALLA WALLA. Moving west from Walla Walla through semi-arid agricultural land along Highway 12, it's 45 miles to Pasco – one of the Tri-Cities on the Columbia River.

The Tri-Cities

Pasco (Population 20,000)

Richland (Population 32,300)

Kennewick (Population 42,200)

This is where the Columbia River, coming across the desert from the north, makes a sharp loop and approaches Oregon. It's here too that both the Snake and the Yakima Rivers enter the Columbia. There's lots of water in this area, enough to satisfy hordes of boaters, swimmers, waterskiers and fishermen. Despite abundant water, the desert looms beyond. But because of the water, much of that desert has been converted to fields of potatoes, alfalfa, truck gardens and orchards of apples and cherries. And irrigation has made this the "Heart of Washington's Wine Country." More than 24 vineyards and wineries are in and around this near-metropolis.

Pasco is the smallest of the three cities, perhaps the least affluent. Much of the agricultural workforce lives here. Plan to stop at **Sacajawea State Park**, three miles southeast of Pasco on Highway 12. Here, where the Snake flows into the Columbia, was a resting place for Lewis and Clark and for the Shoshone woman guide, Sacajawea.

Richland is the middle-sized community, the most well-off of the three. It shows in terms of tourist amenities. This is where much of the manpower comes from to manage nuclear activity, energy production, computers and associated industry.

Just north of Richland on the Columbia is the huge Hanford Nuclear Power Plant. At **Plant 2 Visitor's Center** the mysteries of nuclear power and how it compares with other sources of energy are described. They're not always open. Call first, ☎ 509-372-5860.

Kennewick, the largest town, is supported by power production, chemical processing and agriculture – activities all three towns have in common.

Kennewick is also the place to board boats going up the Columbia, Snake or Yakima Rivers. It's also the site of the **Oasis Waterworks**, where kids will be in heaven. Oasis has 11 exciting water slides, including a Rolling Rapids River ride and a Flash Flood ride. Food is abundant at concession stands and the management promises family fun for everyone. ☎ 509-735-7796.

RECENT HISTORY OF THE AREA. It was WWII, namely the atom bomb, that put this area on the map. People from all over the U.S. were brought here around 1943. Engineers, laborers, physicists, chemists, architects, electricians and carpenters arrived on the scene for a mysterious job. Security was intense and few of the workers knew what they were working on – except that it was a war effort.

In time they found out. It was the atom bomb. Now, peaceful nuclear activities go on and many scientists still work here.

What happens to the radioactive wastes that have accumulated? According to the U.S. Department of Energy, waste is safely stored in "double shell tanks" and placed underground.

OTHER FORMS OF ENERGY – GOOD WINE. In almost any direction from the Tri-Cities, wineries are to be found, at least two dozen of them. **The Bookwalter Winery**, ☎ 509-547-8571, is on Highway 395 north of Pasco. In their tasting room, visitors can sample Cabernets, Merlots, Chardonnays, Rieslings, etc. **Gordon Brothers**, ☎ 509-547-6224, overlooking the Snake River N.E. of Pasco, produces an excellent variety. So does **Preston Wine Cellars**, five miles north of Pasco on Highway 395. They have an attractive wine tasting room looking out on their vineyards. Preston grows award-winning dry reds, dry whites, rosés and blushes. Visit the **Chateau Gallant Winery**, ☎ 509-545-9570, east of Pasco on Highway 124. Try **Columbia Crest Winery**, ☎ 509-545-

2061, on Highway 221 S.W. of town. They have thousands of acres of vineyards.

ACCOMMODATIONS. Cavanaugh's Columbia Center in Kennewick, 1101 N. Columbia Center Blvd., ☎ 509-783-0611, is moderately expensive. **Clearwater Inn**, Kennewick, 5616 Clearwater Ave., ☎ 800-424-1145, is new and centrally located, with moderate prices. **Tapadera Budget Inn**, Kennewick, ☎ 800-722-8277, is at 330A N. Ely. Inexpensive to moderate.

King City Truck Stop, in Pasco on Highway 395, is one mile north of I-82, ☎ 509-547-3475. It has a restaurant and "Truckers Lounge." Inexpensive. **Thunderbird Motel**, Pasco, 414 W. Columbia St., ☎ 509-547-9506, moderate, is downtown, across the street from the acclaimed Farmer's Market.

The Best Western Tower Inn, Richland, 1515 George Washington Way, ☎ 800-635-3980, is the largest conference hotel in Richland, with restaurant and lounge. Moderate to expensive. **Shilo Inn Rivershore**, Richland, 50 Comstock, ☎ 509-946-4661, lies on the banks of the Columbia River. Moderate.

The *Tourist Guide International for Central Washington* will list other accommodations in the area and there are many. But please note that the Tri-Cities can be confusing to drive around. There are bridges to be crossed, intersecting freeways and ambiguous turnoffs. Study a map of the area and call to get directions.

DINING. For elegant dining in Kennewick go to **Cavanaugh's Landing**, 1101 N. Columbia Center Blvd. Moderate to expensive. For barbecued ribs, visit **Roy's Western Smorgy**, 1400 Columbia Center Blvd. Inexpensive. For steaks cooked over a mesquite fire, step into **TS Cattle Co**. on 6515 Clearwater in Kennewick. Moderate.

In Pasco, a nice restaurant that offers relaxed dining in fashionable surroundings is **Rosso's Ristorante**, at the Red Lion Inn, 2525 N. 20th Ave. Moderate to expensive.

In Richland, enjoy Thai food at **Emerald of Siam**, 1314 Jadwin Ave. They serve authentic Thai food at its best. Moderate to expensive.

For further dining, consult the Tri-Cities Dining Guide in the *Tourist Guide International for Central Washington*.

FROM THE TRI-CITIES. And now we come to a place where agriculture is sustained by a benevolent climate and plenty of irrigation water, growing melons, hops, grapes, tomatoes, asparagus and huge quantities of apples. This is the Yakima Valley and the town of Yakima. It lies 82 miles west of the Tri-Cities on Highway 12.

Yakima

Population 55,000

This city where the sun shines 300 days a year, so they say, is where the business of agriculture overpowers everything else. Therein lies its attraction.

For the curious who want to see how America is fed, this is the place. Spend a little time driving through the surrounding farm country and, in season, buy fresh produce at the roadside stands. Then ask the **Visitor's Bureau**, 10 N. 8th Street, ☎ 509-575-1300, for advice on seeing how the produce is processed and shipped.

While in town, ask about riding the vintage **trolley** that moves about town and into some of the farming areas. ☎ 509-575-1700. Plan to visit the **Yakima Mall**, a multilevel area of 650,000 square feet. Escalators and elevators deliver folks to retail stores and outlets of every description.

AT A DISTANCE FROM YAKIMA. To reach the **Yakima Canyon,** get off the freeway that runs between Yakima and Ellensburg (39 miles), drive the old canyon road and stop for a picnic – or perhaps float down a portion of the Yakima River on a raft, canoe or inner tube. This is popular with locals.

ACCOMMODATIONS AND DINING. The Bali Hai Motel, 710 N. 1st St., ☎ 509-452-7178, Inexpensive. **Travelodge**, 110 S. Naches, ☎ 509-457-7151. Moderate. **Cavanaugh's at Yakima Center**, 607 E. Yakima Ave., ☎ 509-248-5900. Restaurant and entertainment. Moderate to expensive. **Red Carpet Motor Inn**, 1608 Fruitvale Blvd., ☎ 509-457-1131. Inexpensive.

To dine with a view, visit the **Whistlin Jack Lodge,** 13 miles north of town on Highway 12. They serve award-winning cuisine among the pines along the Naches River. Moderate to expensive. For music and dancing, go to **Libby's Restaurant** at Cavanaugh's.

Moderate. Get fine steaks at **Stuart Anderson's Black Angus**, 501 N. 1st St. Moderate. There are plenty of other choices in town.

FROM YAKIMA. If Seattle is a destination (144 miles), go north on I-82, then I-90. It's a beautiful, direct trip that takes you through Cle Elum and its scenic lake, then over 3,022-foot Snoqualmie Pass to Seattle.

But if you are fascinated by the Columbia River, take the road back down to Highway 12 for Toppenish, then go south through Goldendale on Highway 97. From Yakima to the Columbia River, it's 83 miles.

Goldendale

Population 3,300

From Toppenish, headquarters for the Yakima Indian Reservation, (a million acres or more), the road runs through scenic wooded country and over a 3,000-foot pass into Goldendale. This is an attractive farming town just 10 miles from the Columbia River and Maryhill State Park. Goldendale is home to the **Goldendale Observatory State Park**, which is one mile north of town on Columbus Ave. The park has a 24½-inch reflecting telescope, one of the biggest in existence. Smaller telescopes are on display too. Some are available for public use. The Observatory is not always open. Call first at ☎ 509-773-4141.

Visit the **Klickitat County Museum**, at 127 W. Broadway, to see pioneer and Indian artifacts, ☎ 509-773-4303.

ACCOMMODATIONS AND DINING. Far Vue Motel, with a restaurant, is at 808 Simcoe Dr., ☎ 509-773-5881. Moderate. **Ponderosa Motel**, 775 E. Broadway, ☎ 509-773-5842, is inexpensive. There are restaurants nearby.

FROM GOLDENDALE. Ten miles south of Goldendale, the Columbia River comes into view. Maryhill State Park is located on the arid banks here and to the east and west the river stretches into the distance.

The Columbia River

It's hard to speak of the Upper Columbia River without referring again to its lower reaches where it empties into the sea at Astoria, Oregon. A little history may help.

In 1792, a fur trading sea captain named Robert Gray was exploring the Pacific Northwest coast when he came upon a large river. He named it the Columbia, after his ship. I'm not sure how far he ascended the river but he certainly put it on the map, which helped two later explorers, Lewis and Clark. These were the men President Jefferson sent across an uncharted continent in 1804-06 and who travelled down the Snake, then the Columbia, all the way to the Pacific Ocean.

Following Lewis and Clark, in the 1840's and 50's, pioneer families following the Oregon Trail descended the Columbia as well – often on perilous rafts. They were hardy souls.

Now, 200 years later, it's possible to board small ships and do the entire navigable length of the Columbia and the Snake, from the ocean to Hell's Canyon. This is a round-trip cruise, beginning and ending in Portland, that covers nearly 1,000 miles.

You can drive the area and see the important sights. But if you want to cruise the river in a comfortable vessel, to eat well, sleep well and be informed by experts, contact **Alaska Sightseeing Cruise West** at 4th and Battery Bldg., Suite 700, Seattle, WA 98121. ☎ 206-441-8687. Travel agents can help too.

This company uses two ships – the 143-foot *Spirit of Columbia* and the 192-foot *Spirit of 98*. The *Spirit of Columbia* has spring, summer and fall departures, the *Spirit of 98* has fall departures only. Fares vary according to cabin selection but for the eight-day, seven-night voyage – beginning and ending in Portland – fares begin at $1,395. This is what passengers can expect.

Day 1. Cruise the Willamette River from Portland to Columbia.

Day 2. Travel up the Columbia through the magnificent Gorge of Bonneville Dam – the first of eight dams which the ship passes. The vessel stops at **Maryhill Museum**, on the Washington side, 18 miles west of The Dalles. This lonesome mansion, on a high cliff over the Columbia in arid treeless country, was built by an eccentric named Sam Hill. I've heard that he built it for his bride, but that may be hearsay. In any event, he had the mansion landscaped, then filled it with art works, including Rodins, Cezannes, Manets and a collection of photos reflecting Indians in the area.

Just east of Maryhill is another curiosity, a model of England's **Stonehenge**. It's not an exact duplicate, but is close enough to attract gatherings of earth worshipers, who appear en masse when the stars are just right.

Day 3. In the dry, warm sunshine of Eastern Washington you cruise under the bluffs of the Snake River and the rolling **Palouse** country. In this area the ship may make a bow landing so passengers can picnic or swim.

Day 4. Lewiston, Idaho. This is as far as cruise vessels can go. Here, passengers take small jet boats up into the **Hells Canyon** region.

Day 5. Passengers are taken to **Walla Walla Whitman Mission**, to **Fort Walla Walla** and to one of Washington's premier wineries.

Day 6. Downriver to **Hood River**, in the heart of the Gorge. From here trips are made by private railroad car into rich orchard lands.

Day 7. All the way downriver to **Astoria**. Here, the ship docks right downtown and passengers are taken to nearby **Fort Clatsop** and to **Oregon beaches**. A Captain's Dinner is held this night.

Day 8. Return to Portland.

Everyone I've talked to who has taken this trip is enthusiastic. Food and cabins are reported as excellent, with the lectures entertaining and informative.